D0477510

SHOOTING AT CLAYS

SHOOTING at CLAYS

ALAN JARRETT

STANLEY PAUL

LONDON SYDNEY AUCKLAND JOHANNESBURG

Stanley Paul & Co. Ltd

An imprint of the Random Century Group
20 Vauxhall Bridge Road
London SW1V 2SA

Random Century Australia (Pty) Ltd
20 Alfred Street, Milsons Point, Sydney 2061

Random Century New Zealand Limited
PO Box 40–086, Glenfield, Auckland 10

Random Century South Africa (Pty) Ltd
PO Box 337, Bergvlei 2012, South Africa

First published 1991

Set in Ehrhardt by Speedset Ltd, Ellesmere Port

Printed and bound in Great Britain by
Clays Ltd, St. Ives PLC

A catalogue record for this book is available
from the British Library

ISBN 0 09 174813 5

Contents

Acknowledgements

I should like to record my appreciation to the following for assistance during the preparation of this book: Brian Hammond (Development Officer, CPSA); George Wallace (Firearms Officer, BASC); David Peel (Gun Sales Manager, Browning Sports); Mervyn Funnell; George Digweed; Ken Harman; Glen Adaway; Dave Peckham; Linda Savage; Ian Marsden; Andy Austin and John Grice. I should also like to thank the proprietors of the following clubs/shooting grounds for allowing me free access for photographic purposes: Kent WCA; Southdown SGC (Sussex); Market Harborough GC (Leicester); Thurlaston GC (Leicester); Garlands SG (Staffordshire); Kingsferry GC (Kent) and Maryland & District GC (Essex) and any others whom I may have inadvertently omitted. Special thanks go to the CPSA for supplying me with copies of their Rules and Regulations for all the major clay pigeon disciplines and for allowing me to quote freely from these publications. CPSA Publications Numbers 8–15 are available from CPSA Headquarters at 107 Epping New Road, Buckhurst Hill, Essex IG9 5TQ and I strongly recommend that shooters interested in an individual discipline obtain a copy of the relevant publication.

Introduction

In my first full-length book, *Wildfowling – One Winter's Tale*, I considered some aspects of the sport of wildfowling, despite its popularity still essentially a minority pursuit amongst the proponents of sporting shotgun shooting. Yet the fact that this tome extended to some 55,000 words on one element of the sport without remotely putting the subject to rest speaks volumes for the complexities which govern not only wildfowling but all other features of shotgun shooting as well. The various branches of the sport include wildfowling, rough shooting, game shooting, pest control, wood-pigeon shooting and clay-pigeon shooting, each in their turn subdivided many times over. The fact that there are so many fundamental variables in even hitting a target consistently, quite aside from questions of fieldcraft – a vital ingredient in the pursuit of live quarry – ensures that people like me will have plenty of use for our pens for some considerable time to come.

Man's desire to hunt is an instinct as old as mankind itself, and still persists in a great many of us. Today, of course, the chief motivation is sport, the acquisition of food being of rather lesser importance. But hunting remains a pitting of wits against a wily quarry, which is why modern-day man still enjoys the chase.

Yet man has happily 'plinked' at inanimate targets too, almost since he first learned to hunt, in order to retain a good eye and a steady arm; few of us will deny the pleasurable childhood memories of pelting chance targets, live or otherwise, with improvised missiles, and the absolute delight at every hit. Such prowess gained at an early age serves us well as we grow older, providing the perfect coordination of hand and eye so vital for success at bat and ball games, or darts – or indeed the shooting of moving targets.

The birth of the clay pigeon during the 1880s, in the basic form in which we know it today, may have been a response to that youthful desire to 'plink'. Or perhaps it was a response to a desire to perfect field skills. Whatever the reason, the sport has grown and blossomed until it now occupies a substantial place alongside such stalwarts as game shooting in terms of participation and support. It is probably unique among shotgun sports in attracting either absorbed interest or total indifference in near equal amounts. There are no moral issues to trouble the clay shooter, no shedding of blood or displacement of fauna to antagonise those opposed to other forms of shooting. If there are any stumbling blocks to continued growth then they are mostly environmental, noise and lead pollution presently being at the top of the list. Both are being increasingly addressed by the administration of this branch of the sport.

The purpose of this book is to take a close look at every facet of shooting at clays. It examines the role of clay shooting in the shotgunners' world of today, and within that the interrelation between clay shooting and many other facets of sport; the relevance of any relationship between clay targets and live-quarry shooting; and, crucially, the seemingly irresistible attraction of the clay-shooting ground combined with the fulfilment of seeing a swiftly flying object disintegrate into tiny pieces. Of equal importance is the subject of competitive clay shooting and its effect on every aspect of the sport – from the targets themselves to the guns – an effect which is far more widespread than many people would have us believe. There are chapters on the various clay-shooting disciplines, many of which are totally divorced from each other with only the target itself offering any common ground. The different competitive elements may seem extremely complex at first glance, but they can in essence be divided into three groups: Sporting (which includes both English and FITASC); Skeet (which includes English, ISU and NSSA); and Trap (which includes Down-the-Line – in its turn sub-divided several times over – Automatic Ball Trap, Olympic Trap, Universal Trench and ZZ). There are inevitably certain similarities within these divisions and where these occur the reader is advised to cross-refer. The opening chapters in each section – English Sporting, English Skeet and Down-the-Line – are comprehensive, dealing with every aspect of the chosen discipline, and thereafter the sub-divisions follow on naturally. The technicalities relating to layouts and the individual disciplines are provided early in each chapter and line drawings and photographs are used to illustrate points in the text.

The instructional aspects of each chapter are of necessity rudimentary, as they must be in a book of this type. Readers wishing to find individual expert advice on any discipline are advised to consult one of the books listed in the Bibliography, many of which are written by acknowledged experts. Better still, a visit to a reputable shooting school will be money well spent.

At the highest level clay shooters now aspire to compete for their country in international or Olympic disciplines. This is the ultimate accolade for the competitive shooter; it is a level to which many aspire but only a tiny number actually rise. I take a look at the champion – that special breed of person who can combat the vast odds stacked against him and still win through.

Finally there is the future of the sport to be considered, a matter of especial relevance in view of environmental pressures. Whether you be shooting prince or pauper the fascination of clay shooting is all-embracing, and I can think of few who have failed to succumb to its charms.

No facet of shotgun shooting can be deemed totally straightforward and in this clay shooting is no exception. It is all about enjoyment, at its most basic level, and about competing, with ultimate success in mind, at the highest level; ranged in between there will be different levels of interest and commitment. As an author it is not my intention to make the sport seem unnecessarily complex, but neither is it wise to gloss over its complexities in order to present it too simplistically. Clay shooting, when viewed as an overall concept, *is* complex and diverse; it is as interesting and varied as any sport can be, and it is also powerfully addictive and will encourage the shooter to pursue it, often to the very limit of his pocket.

In a book which sets out to explain the sport rather than teach the reader how to shoot, it is impossible to offer more than guidelines; but I hope the potential shooter will find that *Shooting at Clays* is the definitive reference work to which he can turn when in need of further guidance.

ABBREVIATIONS

The following abbreviations are used throughout the book:

ABT   Automatic Ball Trap.

BASC   British Association for Shooting and Conservation.

CLA   Country Land Owners' Association.

CPSA   Clay Pigeon Shooting Association.

DTL   Down-the-Line.

FITASC   Fédération Internationale de Tir aux Armes Sportives de Chasse.

ISU (UIT)   International Shooting Union.

OT   15-Trap Olympic Trench (or Trap).

UT   5-Trap Universal Trench.

Club membership
cards

1 The Role of Clay Shooting

The role of the clay pigeon in the shooting world is becoming increasingly important as we near the end of the twentieth century. Indeed, for many people it is an integral component of their sport – even where clays themselves are not the primary target. At first glance this may seem to be a contradiction in terms, but in fact clay shooting now fulfils a variety of roles and as a result is of some importance in any overall consideration of shotgun sports.

The Firearms (Amendment) Act, 1988, has in effect completely changed the emphasis of shotgun ownership: pre-enactment in 1989 it was the right of every individual (assuming that they were not debarred for some reason or other, such as a criminal conviction) to hold a shotgun certificate, and to own and thereafter use such a weapon in a place where they had a lawful right to do so; now, any individuals wishing to obtain a shotgun certificate must first satisfy the chief officer of police in their district that they have 'just cause' within the meaning of the 1988 Act. It therefore follows that club membership, be it a clay-pigeon shooting club or some other type of organisation, goes a good way towards satisfying the police as to a person's honourable intentions. I firmly believe that as time goes by it will become increasingly difficult to obtain a shotgun certificate without at least first demonstrating membership of a *bona fide* shooting club.

Theoretical considerations apart, what actual physical impact is made by the clay pigeon on the modern-day shooting scene? In the earliest days, once the novelty value had worn off, the clay was seen by many shooters as an ideal way of acquiring much-needed practice in preparation for any forthcoming encounters with a live quarry; this still holds good today, although the percentage of clay shooters using the genre exclusively for practise is bound to continue to fall as its overall popularity increases. However, the clay target still fulfils an important role in offering inanimate alternatives for the live-quarry shooter attempting to hone his technique in preparation for either a new shooting season or a special occasion, such as a holiday in pursuit of game. There are few things more disheartening than to start out on an eagerly awaited season only to find that you are shooting like an absolute duffer; some timely practice during the interim period can only do good, and may even eradicate completely those periodic losses of form.

Broadly speaking, any practice at all is good therapy, the best Shots (by 'best' I mean the most consistently accurate over a given period) invariably being those who shoot most often. It often transpires that the casual Shot will miss a high percentage of birds which come his way, and although it would never do to hit absolutely everything it is nevertheless a source of some dismay when too many fly on. So potting away at a few clays, whether this be at a shooting ground proper or from a trap set up at the local farm, is to be advised whenever practical. Of course, one of the great advantages associated with such practice is the ability to tackle virtually any target. The Gun is able to work on a specific weakness to a far greater extent than he ever could in the field. (This aspect of clay shooting will be considered in more detail later.)

The percentage of clay shooters who pursue this side of shotgun shooting to the exclusion of all else continues to grow. There are various reasons for this. The relative dearth of easy access to live quarry in some areas is one highly relevant factor; if the Gun finds himself enamoured with shooting as a sport but severely restricted by a lack of opportunity in the field, then the clay target may offer the only answer. Others may simply enjoy clay shooting for what it is: they may enjoy the ready and easy access to sport and the camaraderie which often exists in smaller clubs, and may also find the lack of pressure and responsibility in casual shooting participation a great tonic and relaxant. Yet again, a percentage of clay shooters do not shoot any live quarry at all, on moral grounds – they enjoy the skill and marksmanship inherent in competent participation in the sport, but do not wish to kill anything in the process.

The competitive role is of growing importance, too. No doubt this is rooted in far-off days when gentlemen wagered one against another on the number of hapless feathered corpses they could accumulate in the field of combat (see the chapter on ZZ shooting). Man is a naturally competitive creature in the main and clay shooting is an ideal way of satisfying such a craving; there is now diversification into an almost bewildering range of 'disciplines' to cater for all manner of tastes and for all degrees of skill, from the Novice right through to the potential Olympic Champion.

But of all its different roles, clay shooting is probably seldom so important as when it is used to accommodate the newcomer to the sport. This is especially true today, when the circumstances of most shooting enthusiasts are so different from those of their predecessors. In former times the great majority of shooting folk came to the sport from a rural or sporting background; in many instances the ways of the countryside and of sport had been part of their upbringing, so that most shooters were aware from an early age of sporting constraints and of their responsibilities to both quarry and fellow sportsmen. Almost invariably shooting folk were caring, responsible and above all safe. Today this is no longer true to the same degree. Many adults come into the sport without a thorough grounding in sporting safety and etiquette. It is here that clay shooting has such an important role to play. Despite the larger number of armed participants present at any one time, the clay-shooting ground is one of the safest shooting venues to be found anywhere. In fact, clay shooters are safety conscious almost to the point of paranoia – which is as it should be.

Father/daughter tuition

2 Equipment

The term 'clay pigeon' dates back to the earliest days of competitive target shooting. Of course, things were very different in the final decades of the nineteenth century, when weaponry and ammunition were less efficient and targets were very much alive. Gentlemen shooters vied with each other to pot as many pigeons as they could, as the unfortunate creatures – invariably minus their tail feathers, which had been judiciously removed beforehand in order to create the ultimate in erratic flight – fluttered from their tiny imprisoning chambers to offer shots that were scarcely the ultimate in terms of demanding sporting targets. The idea that the bird should be dropped within a set perimeter brought a greater challenge to the sport, the Shot needing to be far quicker on to his birds. The difficulties inherent in providing enough real pigeons led to other birds such as starlings often being used as a worthy, if not quite equivalent, substitute. The sport continued among the gentry of the day, but the problems in procuring live targets, and the dubious morality of shooting captive birds the instant they were airborne, meant that the sport of live-pigeon shooting was overtaken by a more challenging and socially acceptable alternative. Glass balls – later filled with feathers as a foil against cheating in competitions – fired from a crude launching apparatus, arrived on the scene during the 1870s and gained a certain popularity; in some cases big competitions took place involving fantastic sums of money, while the numbers of glass balls broken could be measured in tons.

Today the shooting of live captive birds is quite rightly illegal in Great Britain and in many other countries, although its memory lingers on in the shooting of the artificial winged ZZ targets, where archaic pigeon-shooting principles have been retained. These include a series of traps from which the target might 'fly', and the perimeter fence within which the 'dead' target must fall (see Chapter 16). Live pigeons and glass balls are out, clay pigeons most definitely in. The first modern clay pigeon was in existence by the late 1880s, and the sport has steadily gained in popularity until nowadays it enjoys near cult status. Most importantly, it is no longer the exclusive preserve of the rich who could afford to wager fabulous sums on the outcome of some competition. It is now accessible, in one form or another, to anyone who chooses to have a go.

THE TARGET

The actual 'clay', as the target is universally known, is no more made of clay than it is shaped like a pigeon. In short, it in no way resembles a bird. The actual physical make-up varies from one manufacturer to another though it will usually be a mixture of chalk and pitch – sprayed the appropriate colour if anything other than black is required. The modern clay pigeon in fact needs to be a precisely engineered and constructed piece of hardware: it must be strong enough to withstand the not inconsiderable shock of being launched from its 'trap' at speeds of up to 80 m.p.h.; at the same time it needs to be fragile enough to break if hit by even a single pellet – not as easy a formula to arrive at as it might seem at first glance. Over the years the quality of clays has varied a great deal, some manufacturers producing targets which have been too hard. There is nothing more infuriating in clay-shooting circles than to walk through the target landing area and to come across a succession of intact targets which have holes shot clean through them but which have flown on as if unhit. As the rules of clay shooting cite quite clearly that a discernible piece must be seen to detach itself from the target before it can be credited as a 'kill' (dust or movement from the flight path will not suffice), it is obviously essential that every clay does in fact break when hit. Prizes can, of course, be won or lost on the strength of a single 'kill', and it will do nothing for a shooter's confidence or temper if he is aware that hard targets are being used. Generally, multiple strikes will cause the clay to shatter into myriad pieces, and this is the ideal situation as it proves both satisfying for the shooter and easy work for the person responsible for recording the scores.

Most shooting venues, whether holding an informal get-together or a top-class competition, use the 'standard' clay, in either black or orange (blaze). This will be 120 mm in diameter and around 26 mm in height and is in essence not dissimilar to an inverted ashtray; various colours may be used, blaze being the most common for such disciplines as Trap, where a black clay may prove less easy to pick out against an obscuring background. The standard clay is versatility itself and may be presented in a wide variety of situations and circumstances guaranteed to test the Shot to the maximum; almost all traps are designed with these clays in mind, so that some modifications may be necessary on occasion in order to throw non-standard targets.

Other variations also exist, designed to increase the permutations available to the shoot organiser, although these are basically confined to the area of Sporting shooting. The 'midi' is a 90 mm target which can often completely fool the shooter who fails to spot the change in size and therefore speed and flight and to make the necessary adjustments to the manner in which he addresses the target. The 'mini' is a 60 mm target and is as swift as a tiny black wasp; it can sometimes provide the ultimate test for the shooter in terms of speed of swing and range judging. The 'battue' is a near-flat standard-sized clay which is initially very swift but crucially performs some crazy manoeuvres as it slows down. Finally, the 'rabbit' is again standard-sized but tough enough to bounce along the ground without shattering. The permutations and uses are many and varied, and will be discussed in more detail later. Here we can at least begin to gain an insight into some of the complexities to be encountered in the sport.

Sample clay types: (left to right) mini, midi, standard

THE TARGET LAUNCHER

The target launcher, commonly and hereafter called the 'trap', is in its most basic form a simple enough piece of machinery consisting of a base for fixing on to a rigid position, a powerful spring and an arm upon which the clay will sit until the moment of launch. Actual design varies from one manufacturer to another, but all traps will do a similar job within the set parameters outlined above. The simplest type of trap throws a fairly slow and undemanding clay which rapidly loses momentum before flopping unceremoniously to earth – ideal for the beginner to practise on. (It should not be dismissed contemptuously, for this type of trap has other uses, which will be dealt with later.) This basic design can be enhanced considerably by the addition of an adjustable spring tensioner (to control speed and therefore distance) and arm elevation (which controls height), and with these elementary additions the variety of available targets can be increased many fold. Other specialist Sporting traps can throw high, fast-climbing clays, or be used to launch the rabbit clay along the ground in a series of erratic bounds, and are a valuable constituent part of any large layout.

When it comes to the more specialist disciplines of Skeet, and the even more complex field of Trap, we enter a new world of expensive,

Typical Sporting
trap

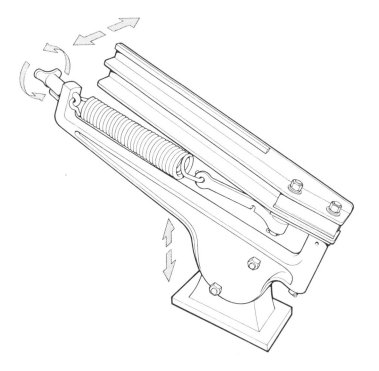

Figure 1 Typical
Sporting trap
showing the basic
adjustments
needed to throw a
variety of target
types

sophisticated machines, many of which are operated and released by mains electricity and microchip technology. In terms of high-tech equipment the modern Trench layout is in a class of its own, and really emphasises how far the sport has evolved. For Skeet a fairly rudimentary single-arm trap will suffice, provided that there is the capacity to alter both speed and elevation, even though such changes will need to be slight in response to changing weather conditions. However, fully automatic magazine-fed traps are increasingly being used. These are great labour savers, although only after an initial high cash outlay on equipment. For Down-the-Line (DTL) even the manually loaded traps – such as the popular Winchester White Flyer – are very expensive, as are such magazine traps as the Farey or Laporte; invariably grounds install a type of trap which will double for both DTL and Automatic Ball Trap (ABT) by the provision of an extra electric motor to give the variable elevation required in ABT at the flick of a switch. For the Trench disciplines the traps need to be of a far simpler design, as they launch clays along a set path from below ground; the short trap arm – to facilitate instant maximum velocity – is one of the most notable features.

GUNS

Having looked at the target end of the sport it is obviously necessary to consider the business end – the gun itself. Basically you can use any

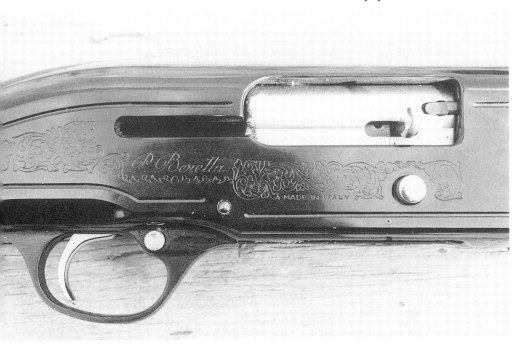

available shotgun for clay shooting, from the cheapest side-by-side, to the semi-automatic, to the most expensive of over-and-under. Indeed, many shooters use their normal field gun for clay shooting, and do fairly well at that. Really the only shotgun which is manifestly unsuitable for clay shooting is the pump-action, because of the slowness in firing the second shot. The popularity of these weapons in the USA is not duplicated on this side of the Atlantic. Yet use of the side-by-side and the semi-auto is confined to a fairly small percentage of serious clay shooters; these are more likely to be found at the small shoot, which often relies for its patronage on a local nucleus of game shooters and friends. Unless there is a special class – such as the side-by-side class at some bigger events – the proportion of people using such weapons at most shoots will be low. Curiously, perhaps, the semi-auto, which lends itself ideally to such disciplines as Sporting and Skeet, does not seem to have the following it once enjoyed.

The over-and-under is the most popular weapon for clay shooting. Fashion may have had an initial impact, but any such influence has long since been outgrown. Pointability, occasioned by the single sighting plane, will generally be excellent, while the greater weight inherent in this sort of design lends itself readily to withstanding the constant recoil suffered by clay shooters. Manufacturers now work hard to produce a range of high-quality over-and-unders which will satisfy every whim of the shooting fraternity. All sectors of the market are catered for, ranging from the £300 gun right through to a top-

Action of the semi-auto

19

Lanber Sporter

quality sidelock weapon costing £4000 or more. Different needs are also borne in mind. Many manufacturers are renowned for their competition-grade guns – Browning and Beretta to name but two – and this means that many specialist weapons for Skeet, Sporting and Trap are made, including a considerable range within these disciplines. The variety of guns can become mind-blowing for the beginner, although the experienced shooter generally knows roughly what he needs and is able to limit his search to a smaller range of weapons.

One of the greatest advances in shotgun manufacture in recent years has been the introduction of the multi-choke facility, available mainly on Sporting-type guns and to a lesser extent on other specialist weapons. It allows the shooter to consider just how to tackle each target, and to adjust his choke accordingly. Of course, this will not necessarily give the multi-choke owner an advantage over the shooter with the fixed chokes, but any option on a gun must be considered a potentially useful facility. Many clay shooters can therefore now use the same weapon for every discipline. Modern Sporting guns are ideal for Skeet in many instances, although Trap shooting presents problems peculiar to this branch of the sport.

CARTRIDGES

Cartridge manufacture has developed to a point where high-performance competition loads are available from many sources, Britain, the USA and various European countries turning out prodigious numbers. It can be said by way of a sweeping generalisation that all good-quality cartridges are by and large pretty much the same, and that individual preferences are often governed by a bias not necessarily related to fact. This is true up to a point, although each cartridge will perform differently – variations in muzzle velocity, for example – and most shooters have their favourites. Cartridge selection is treated with a degree of disdain by many non-competitive clay

shooters, price being the main arbiter in many cases. On the other hand, the competition shooter is likely to be obsessively fussy. Some of the top competition shooters even go to the extreme of having their gun regulated to suit a particular type of cartridge, which one day may well give them a precious edge. Mostly, however, the normal 1 oz load of either 7½, 8 or 9 shot size is used, according to the discipline, variations around this average being confined to specific types of shooting. For example, many shooters used 1¼ oz loads for the sort of long-range targets encountered in FITASC (Fédération Internationale de Tir aux Armes Sportives de Chasse) Sporting, or for ZZ targets. But 1 oz loads are now mandatory for most competitive clay shooting, even if 1⅛ oz loads are still widely used in the field. Cartridges with more 'punch' are often used for long-range second-barrel shots, while harder nickel-coated pellets may be used as a foil against the lack of striking power which may be experienced at long range.

Changeable choke tubes (Browning)

A sample of the wide range of cartridges available

Cartridge prices among all the major brands vary by less than £10 per thousand, with only virtual luxury items such as nickel-coated ones being well outside this range. Non-stop price wars between retailers ensure that prices are kept as low as possible for those buying in bulk – 1000 or more – so that profit margins are kept low and shooters are thus more likely to get better value. This is an important point for those who shoot a great deal. Because only the very best Shots can offset costs with prize money or sponsorship, any shooter who competes regularly is going to spend a fair amount of money over the course of a year on cartridges alone.

CLOTHING

Clothing for exclusive use on the clay-pigeon ground is, like all clothing, partly a matter of taste, although such taste is determined largely by practicalities rather than fashion trends. Clothing must fulfil certain clear-cut functions. Waterproofing and windproofing, with no constriction of movement and therefore of gun-handling, are essential. The universally worn waistcoat – still widely referred to as a Skeet vest – is the outer layer and consists of a sleeveless garment with ample pockets into which can be tumbled at least fifty cartridges. A shoulder patch is usual, invariably made of leather: its purpose is to discourage gun slip on mounting rather than to act as padding. On the shooting ground many shooters will be found wearing similar

garments, dark blue being a common colour. Some quite excellent wind- and water-proof suits are now available, which make all the difference when the weather is at its worst, as no shooter can perform to optimum efficiency when he is cold and wet. Footwear is again a matter of personal choice and will depend on discipline and weather: the Sporting shooter can expect to wallow in mud on occasions and must be prepared; in contrast, many Trap shooters now enjoy the luxury of shooting from covered positions and may therefore wear shoes or trainers. Hats are invariably of the peaked variety. Once again practical considerations rule: a peak keeps both sun and water from the eyes.

Skeet vest, cap, gloves and ear muffs

ACCESSORIES

The shooter's accessories include tinted sunglasses, probably at least two different sorts for highlighting different coloured clays. Blinkers are often added to glasses by Trap shooters in order to help rule out the possibility of distractions, which might mar crucial concentration. Blinkers are more likely to be made from mutilated cartridge boxes than to be purpose-built. Strap-on foot-pads, much favoured by Trap shooters in an effort to avoid those tell-tale black muzzle rings left on shoes by resting the gun in this position in between shots, are commonplace, as is a variety of other aids from bags and gun-slips to snap-caps and cleaning gear.

3 Entering the Sport

There has been a noticeable change in the way in which many people now enter the shooting sports. This applies in some degree to all facets of shooting, but most particularly to clay-pigeon shooting. The traditional route into shooting via family and friends, whereby youngsters would be brought on gradually until they became a permanent part of the set-up, does still hold good today. But there is an increasing number of adults, many of whom may be of mature years, who want to take up the sport. It is to this new class of shooters that much of this chapter, indeed a substantial proportion of this book, is directed.

THE RURAL SHOOTER

Until perhaps the last twenty years the essential hard core of shooters was made up of those with some sort of rural background, or at least strong rural ties. True, plenty of urban dwellers shot, but in essence the bulk of devotees had that firm rural base. Those living close to the land see Nature's creatures as part of the harvest which man can glean from the countryside, and sport, in particular sporting shooting, has evolved as a way of country life. In my boyhood and youth, through the late 1950s and early 1960s, every country person seemed to have access to a gun; there would be one standing in the corner of every kitchen, and even in the pub on a Sunday lunch-time it was not uncommon to see a small clutch of assorted guns and bags and perhaps even a dead bird or rabbit surreptitiously tucked away behind a back door. In short, it was a way of life for a large number of people. In addition, anything shot was often a valuable contribution to the table at a time when there was still the memory of the deprivations of war rationing.

Rural people were traditionally gun orientated, and even if some of the weapons in use were fearsome old wrecks which always seemed as likely to harm the shooter as the target, there was a deep respect for, and affinity with, the destructive power of the shotgun. Safety, even if it may have seemed a little slapdash, was closely attended to. The comparative dearth of gun accidents in that period was undoubted

testimony to the fact that everyone appreciated the potential danger of what they were about. The family/friend method of schooling in shooting ways was easy-going and essentially informal; yet woe betide anyone who transgressed. Many a boxed ear or period of gunless penance enforced the unwritten code of 'Never, ever let your gun, pointed be at anyone'! Even if many rural folk of the period were vagabond poachers and slaughterers of game, whether sitting or flying, in response to a need for protein, there were always the unwritten codes: of safety; of good behaviour; of etiquette, and of respect not just for one's fellow shooter but for the quarry, too.

The rural shooting scene is a traditional breeding ground for up-and-coming shots

The earliest competitive clay shooters mostly came from this stock. They were engrained with the old ways, and whether or not they were excellent Shots when on the clay circuit, they were always and above all else gentlemen; whether they spoke with a Fenlander's burr or with a plum in the mouth made no difference.

Competition was little excuse to forget long-established principles, and if the other man won, it was because he was the better man on the day, not because the scorer was blind or did not understand the rules, or because it was less windy when old so-and-so shot. Of course, the fabulous prizes often available at today's big shoots were not on offer then, but had they been I firmly believe that the attitude of the great majority of shooters would have changed very little.

There was seldom any formal training. Today's shooting schools and gun clubs were unheard of. Considering the lack of training and the almost archaic guns and ammunition with which they tried to perform, there was a large nucleus of remarkably efficient shots. Today the guns are first class, as is the ammunition, and there is probably more money around to finance both. If the old rural shooter had an aim, aside from putting something in the pot, it was to perform well when pitted against his fellows, with the national team badge or Olympic medal the ultimate glory. Yes, it was always good to win, but not the be all and end all it sometimes seems today. Fortunately, many shooters do still enter the sport by the traditional route. And in addition to the informal training and indoctrination outlined above they now have the considerable benefits of the latest in modern shooting hardware and access to sound professional tuition. The competitive shooter of today is a very precisely trained and capable clay-busting individual, which may explain why so many first-class young shooters are coming through to challenge their seniors. It bodes very well for the future of the sport.

THE NOUVEAU SHOOTER

Shooting in the late 1980s and through into the 1990s has become hugely popular, keenly pursued by a large section of the population who are not countrymen even if they actually live in the country or have countryside affiliations. This, of course, is not meant as a criticism, and most certainly countrymen born and bred do not have a monopoly on the right to bear arms. Nevertheless, the potential shooter, who comes to the sport perhaps later on in life, will undoubtedly face many problems which, for the traditional shooter, do not exist. It is largely in response to this emergent class of sportsman that modern training facilities have evolved. Indeed, if the shooting school had to rely on the country lad for trade then it would very soon go broke.

Hitherto, the relative lack of opportunity to shoot over land was perhaps one of the prime inhibiting factors in determining who would actually take up the sport. Those with a rural upbringing were likely to have a better chance of establishing the necessary contacts in the countryside which would allow them access to shoot, and from this it is logical to assume that for those without contacts the difficulties associated with getting into shooting would have multiplied many times. This does not apply to quite the same degree today, when shooting opportunities come in many forms. Not that there is any more land available for shooting. It is indeed quite the reverse as more and more countryside is developed. But the whole shooting ethic has changed, and is changing still.

One of the most significant changes can be summed up in one word – money. Shooting is now much more money-orientated than ever before: land that hitherto was not accessible at any price now often does have a price; sold days play a major role in the running of many shoots, including a fair proportion of the bigger game shoots which in many cases could not exist without a regular injection of outside cash; clubs and syndicates of all sorts and sizes now exist with the sole aim of providing shooting for members; and where cash is not an inhibiting factor the shooter is able to buy himself sport. For those who do not wish to shoot live quarry the proliferation of clay-shooting facilities knows no bounds. Here again money is the key to participation, for as long as the cash is available any shooter can shoot as often as he has a mind to.

For many nouveau shooters the sport is a relaxing and therapeutic pastime; if it were not shooting, then perhaps it would be golf or windsurfing or some other open-air pursuit. Clay shooting is particularly attractive in that it is readily and easily available in almost any part of the country. There are none of the moral considerations which beset some people when they consider shooting live quarry; the same degree of marksmanship and general competence with a gun will be required whether the target is real or artificial, and it is becoming very 'hip' to be involved in a pastime which enjoys an increasingly high public profile, as clay shooting most certainly does.

TRAINING

For those lacking a rural shooting upbringing, clay shooting is in many ways an ideal introduction to the sport, not least because of the safety aspect. Clay shooters are, almost without exception, intensely safety conscious, and it is therefore a pleasure to shoot in their company. Over the years I have seen some appalling examples of carelessness with a gun in the field. Although these were very few and far between they were all avoidable. In each case the consequences could have been dire. Such incidents usually occur when the shooter has had insufficient grounding in the fundamental basics of the sport, and while I would not venture to say that all are perpetrated by non-countrymen, this is often the case. On the reverse side of the coin, unsafe gun handling is virtually unheard of on the clay-shooting ground, despite the very wide cross-section of people taking part. High standards are demanded and attained and any transgressor is dealt with quickly and firmly.

For the complete novice clay shooter safety precautions are the very first thing to be learnt. No shooting instructor worthy of the name will even consider letting loose an inexperienced Gun without first drumming into him the fundamental precept that guns can be very dangerous and can easily maim or even kill. It is crucial that the shooter quickly gets into good habits. The basic common-sense precautions include:

Typical Trap
shooter's waiting
position with gun
open

- Always carry the gun open, with no cartridges in the chambers.
- Never point a gun in the direction of another person, even when it is known to be unloaded.
- Never turn from a clay-shooting stand with a closed gun.
- Always check the barrels for obstructions before loading.

These are among the most fundamental of safety measures, and the newcomer who quickly learns to appreciate them will more rapidly progress with his tuition.

The actual choice of gun will be considered later, when discussing the individual disciplines. For now it will suffice to look at the sort of tuition available to the would-be shooter who has yet to acquire his own weapon. Most shooting schools have a range of guns from which to choose, and unless the pupil is of extraordinary physical dimensions or has some major disability, it will be possible to come up with one which will be close to a reasonable fit. Obviously this is not an ideal scenario, but it will teach the pupil safety and the rudiments of hitting a moving target. Fine-tuning can come later, once the shooter has moved on to his own gun. To begin with the student needs to master all the apparent complexities of shooting: how to stand; how to hold the gun; how to move correctly relative to the various target types on offer, and many other factors as and when they occur.

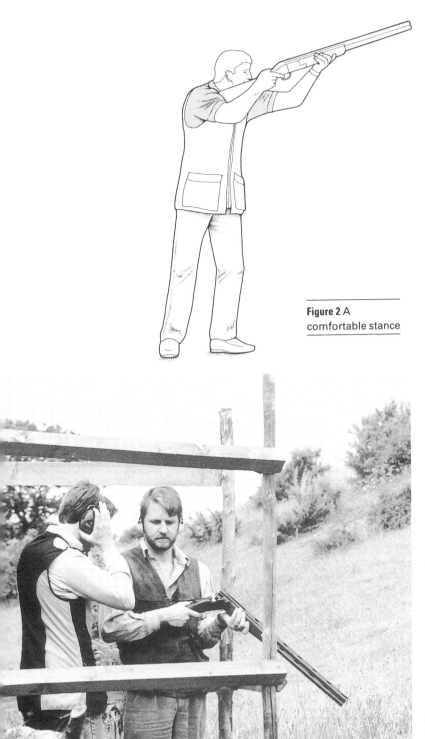

Figure 2 A
comfortable stance

'Now listen!'

As the illustrations show, there are certain basic prerequisites which need to be mastered before the art of hitting a flying target can be mastered. While for the experienced Shot the concept of shooting in front of a moving target is elementary, for the beginner it is not so easy to coordinate eye and body to carry out the multiplicity of functions necessary to succeed. Initial instruction invariably calls for the shooter to shoot with the gun pre-mounted – much as the Trap shooter habitually does. This immediately obviates some of the newcomer's major problems, which arise from the difficulty of mounting correctly and thereafter hitting the target. The shooter will be taught safety, stance, gun mount and swing, and should soon be hitting the more straightforward type of target.

The novice will be well advised to beware of the sort of *ad hoc* assistance often offered (in a quite well-meaning and genuine sort of way) by different Guns, some of which may be contradictory and therefore confusing. If you want to learn quickly and thoroughly, the shooting school, with its trained instructors, is the place to go. Although the initial cost may seem fairly high, it will be cost effective in the long run if it saves months, perhaps years, of frustration and disappointment.

Even the more experienced shooter, conditioned to self-train through constant and continual practice, can benefit from tuition. Self-training is a technique which works up to a point, and as long as no constant flaw exists in the basic shooting style there should be few problems. Unfortunately, where a shooter, even an experienced one, develops a flaw in technique, he is often the last person to see it. This can develop without any obvious reason. If it is not detected and corrected it can lead to a ruinous spell of shooting which will have disastrous consequences for the competition shooter. Alternatively, many shooters have a weakness which they find hard to eradicate (for example, in my own case I am weakest at high on-coming targets), and no amount of practice or self-assessment can cure the problem. At such times it really does make sense to go to a shooting school and seek the advice of a trained instructor who will in all probability sort out the problem in double-quick time, often in the course of a single lesson. For the competition shooter, spending probably in excess of £30 per shoot, this really is a cost-effective exercise. It is difficult to understand why such faults develop. Any one of a number of factors is likely to have an effect. Unfortunately we all fall into the trap of self-diagnosis, which often leads us down the slippery slope to worse and worse scores, with all the attendant morale-destroying consequences. It can take a long time to recover from such a spell, and if more experienced shooters could swallow their pride earlier, then they might see a quicker and cheaper improvement.

'Practice makes perfect' is one of those hackneyed sayings which is so often near the truth. Of course, perfect is somewhat over the top, but what regular practice does do is hone whatever ability may be possessed to its very limit. The mediocre Shot will probably never improve to the very top standard, simply because it is beyond his capability. But through constant practice he can often remain at a consistent level of performance which will pay dividends when other Shots suffer a fall-off in form. For the really gifted Shot, practice will ensure that loss of form is kept to a minimum, and only by practice can he expect to remain at the top of the tree. It really is horses for courses, with different shooters capable of different levels of performance, and it would be unrealistic for most to aspire to the very highest level just by virtue of constant practice. Practice and tuition will maximise the ability you possess but will not give you that extra flair and talent possessed by the true champion. Fortunately most Shots are realistic enough to have more modest aims, and their training techniques reflect this: most aspire to shoot competently and to hit a reasonable proportion of what they fire at, to compete with a degree of honour against those of like ability, and not to disgrace themselves in exalted company. That said, we have probably said it all.

4 Legal Aspects

The legalities surrounding the ownership of shotguns are fairly straightforward, although there are a few notable points of potential misunderstanding. Essentially, as far as the clay shooter is concerned, the sport has until recently been governed by the Firearms Act, 1968, although the recent addition of the Firearms (Amendment) Act, 1988 has had sweeping effects, many of which are still working their way through the system. Seldom in the annals of shooting sports has a single piece of legislation caused such a furore, for the most part justifiably so. Shooters have been obliged to suffer an ill-conceived piece of legislation, often further aggravated by insensitive handling by certain constabularies, and there can be no denying that the Amendment is a deeply unpopular vehicle towards the tighter control of sporting arms. Sadly, animosity between the police and the law-

Legislation affects
all shooters

abiding sporting community has damaged the respect hitherto felt by the latter towards the former, and we may rue the day when the politicians responded to tabloid newspaper hysteria following a particularly outrageous and horrific crime involving the use of firearms (not, incidentally, a shotgun).

As a result of the Firearms (Amendment) Act, 1988, a number of changes in the law relating to the purchase, acquisition, possession and sale of shotguns came into force on 1 July 1989. The new shotgun controls came into immediate effect for all certificates issued on or after that date, though for certificates issued prior to 30 June 1989 the new controls take effect when those certificates expire. Various separate conditions also apply to individuals whose certificates were issued prior to 30 June 1989; however, because the publication of this book will soon be overtaken by the expiry of all such certificates (they will have expired by 1 July 1992), these aspects will not be dealt with. Readers in need of advice should contact their representative organisation – the British Association for Shooting and Conservation (BASC), Clay Pigeon Shooting Association (CPSA) or some other. The changes in the law relating to the sale of shotgun ammunition also came into effect on 1 July 1989.

WHAT IS A SHOTGUN?

There is now a new definition as to what constitutes a shotgun, and this definition seriously affects the owners of semi-automatic and pump-action weapons. A shotgun is a smooth-bore weapon which meets the following criteria:

(a) It has a barrel length of not less than 24 inches, and a bore of 2 inches or less in diameter.

(b) It does not have a magazine, or has a non-detachable magazine which cannot hold more than two cartridges.

(c) It is not a revolver.

If your gun meets these criteria, then all should be fine. If it does not, the following actions need to be urgently considered because the weapon will be classified as either a firearm or a prohibited weapon; for shotgun owners this will apply mostly to holders of semi-automatic and pump-action weapons. If the gun is not defined as a shotgun, the options are as follows:

(a) Apply for a firearms certificate on the appropriate form available at any police station.

(b) Have the magazine adapted so that it is possible for the weapon to retain shotgun status – this can be carried out by any competent gunsmith for a fee generally well below £50, to include the necessary London or Birmingham Proof House inspection, marking and certification.

(c) Have the gun de-activated. Once again the relevant Proof House will need to attest to this de-activation.

(d) Dispose of the gun by selling to a registered firearms dealer or a firearms certificate holder who is authorised to acquire this type of weapon, or by handing it in to a police station.

APPLICATION FOR A SHOTGUN CERTIFICATE

New certificates will contain a detailed description of all guns held, including any identification numbers, will bear a photograph of the certificate holder, and will include new safe-keeping conditions, designed to ensure the safe custody of shotguns. The certificate application form must be counter-signed by a person of good standing in the community who has been acquainted with the applicant for at least two years; this is generally understood to be a professional person such as a solicitor, doctor or magistrate, although as an acceptance that many ordinary shooting people may not know such a person the Home Office has agreed that various officials of *bona fide* shooting organisations can act as counter-signatories.

There is a new emphasis governing the conditions whereby a shotgun certificate may be issued. A chief officer of police will not be able to grant a shotgun certificate if:

(a) He is not satisfied that the applicant can possess a shotgun without danger to public safety or to the peace.

(b) He is satisfied that the applicant does not have a good reason for possessing, purchasing or acquiring a shotgun (examples of 'good reason' are sporting or competition purposes, the shooting of vermin, and some situations where the gun is not intended for use, such as if it is a family heirloom or part of a collection).

(c) He has reason to believe the applicant is prohibited from possessing a shotgun.

TRANSFER AND SALE OF SHOTGUNS

This concerns the transfer of shotguns between private individuals. 'Transfer' in this context means sale, letting on hire, giving as a gift or lending for a period of more than seventy-two hours. When both parties hold a certificate issued or renewed after 1 July 1989 the following requirements apply:

(a) A person *transferring* a shotgun must enter details of the gun on the new holder's certificate. Within seven days of the transaction he must also send a notice of the transaction to the chief officer of police who issued his shotgun certificate.

(b) A person who *acquires* a shotgun must send a note of the transaction within seven days of the transaction taking place to the chief officer of police who issued the certificate.

(c) The notice sent to the chief officer of police must contain a description (including any indentification number), details of the nature of the transaction and the name and address of the other person involved. This notice must be sent by either registered post or recorded delivery.

Other conditions exist relating to circumstances when either party holds a certificate issued before 30 June 1989.

PURCHASING OF SHOTGUN AMMUNITION

Whatever expiry date exists on the certificate, a current shotgun certificate must be produced in order to purchase ammunition.

SECURITY OF SHOTGUNS

A great deal of fuss is made about this point, with the criteria varying significantly according to which constabulary happens to be involved. Some constabularies make specifications concerning type of security required and these can in extreme cases dictate the scale and type of security, right down to the type of lock on a cabinet and the gauge of steel used in the cabinet's design. Elsewhere there may be strict demands for house security, including specifications relating to the type of window lock and burglar alarm to be fitted. None of these demands has any basis in law and the representative bodies argue quite justifiably that if Parliament did not see fit to include such speci-fications in the Act, then it is most certainly not the place of the police to insert their own specifications. The Act merely dictates that reasonable security be demonstrated in order to ensure the safe custody of guns. Technically this means that there is no need for window locks, burglar alarms or even security cabinets; in practice most reasonable shotgun certificate holders provide a steel cabinet securely fixed to the fabric of the house, and also ensure that such a cabinet is in an unobtrusive place. This is deemed reasonable by most people, and where a constabulary attempts to insist on more, the certificate holder/applicant really should seek further advice – preferably from the BASC, which has a well-versed and effective firearms department. Indeed, this is sound advice for any problem associated with firearms or any other aspect of shotgun usage, for the BASC offers an unparalleled service to its members.

5 The 'Fun' Shooter

Even though competitive clay shooting is very popular, unquestionably the vast majority of active participants in the sport have little or no interest in competition other than in a very low-key, good-natured sort of way. They will want few fancy frills, asking only that the layout is safe and the targets killable.

For the competitive shooter enjoyment and success are indivisibly interlinked, lack of success marring ultimate enjoyment. But the truly casual shooter will have an enjoyable time regardless of competitive success; naturally there will still be that wish to break a few clays, but there is a world of difference between the attitude of those content to break, say, 50 per cent of clays, and those for whom a single missed target over a course of 100 may spell ruination and despair. These are the remarkable extremes encountered within the sport.

HAVE A GO

Enjoyment is fundamental for the great majority of those who shoot. Comparatively few shotgun users shoot for purely professional reasons, the gamekeeper and the pest controller heading what is a short list. Hitherto a considerable number of rurally based people used a gun to augment their diet. But although many people still do so today, there is a crucial difference: the inaccurate Shot is less likely to starve as a result of inefficiency with the gun.

First contacts will leave a lasting impression, and it is therefore crucial that that initial experience proves to be a happy event. Clay shooting must be, and indeed is, readily available to all manner of casual shooters. Many country sports fairs and county shows offer a wide range of events. Low-key sporting shoots will often form the basis of what is available, but other offerings such as flurries, pool shoots and rudimentary down-the-line may be present, too. Crucially the have-a-go stand is always a feature, and it is to this that crowds of eager spectators, often complete novices flock.

The have-a-go stand can be anything the organisers decide. However, it must comprise certain elements if the stand is to be a success. It will need to have both guns and cartridges readily available,

Prize-giving for the successful shooter – Belinda Usher – Ladies Skeet Champion

The have-a-go stand never has a shortage of takers at country fairs

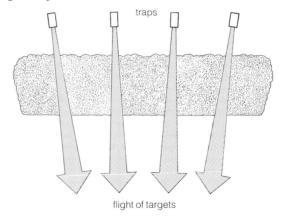

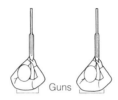

Figure 3 Careful coordination between the Guns is essential when shooting the flurry

because most participants will have neither; there should be a competent adult in charge, capable of providing some elementary coaching for those who need it; the clays thrown should be easy to hit, so that the novice can discover that it is not necessarily that difficult to hit a moving target; and finally, cost should be kept to a minimum – even though clay shooting can scarcely be deemed a cheap pastime, excessive cost at an early stage may prove off-putting. If the person in charge of the stand does a good job, any novice will quickly discover that shooting is safe, relatively painless and thoroughly enjoyable once those small black targets start to break. Thus reassured, the budding clay shooter is increasingly likely to go to such country-orientated events with clay shooting specifically in mind. From becoming a regular participant at the have-a-go stand it is but a short step to acquiring a gun and really getting into some regular clay shooting.

SPORTING FOR FUN

For most casual clay shooters regular clay shooting will take the form of Sporting, a subject of great complexity whose various categories are dealt with in more detail in Chapter 8. For now, suffice it to say that such shoots can provide a mix of targets as varied as the organisers care to make them. The layout may be hard or easy, the permutations being virtually endless. Beyond doubt Sporting is the most difficult of the commonly found disciplines, simply because of its wide variations. As

a result, it is not perhaps the best starting point for the inexperienced Shot who wants to attain a reasonably high standard. The lack of duplication, which makes this discipline so interesting, is one of the reasons why many Shots need to labour over a long period to improve their skill rating.

The flurry is always popular and enjoyable

Of all the disciplines, Sporting most resembles hunting wild quarry. The setting is invariably ultra-rural, with few of the stereotyped concrete layouts so necessary in the more regimented disciplines of Trap and Skeet; the atmosphere at the smaller shoots is light and cheerful, with no pressure on the shooter to perform well. In short, it is the chosen form of clay shooting for a vast army of shooters, the thirty, forty or fifty target shoot being widely popular. Because such a format makes no great demands of the shooter in terms of cost or concentration, it may prove the ideal starting point.

Many such shoots exist solely for the casual shooter. If there is any competition at all, it will usually be for a few trophies. In the summer, when a host of redundant game and wildfowl shooters scour the countryside for a means of keeping their eye in, there is a sharp upturn in the amount of Sporting being shot. For the game shoot or wildfowling club, summer clay shoots may be an important part of the year's itinerary. They also perform an important social function by keeping members in touch with one another and, if the site is an attractive one, offer an enjoyable family day out. For most of the participants, winning is the last thing on their mind.

The lack of inhibition at such venues will be reflected in the shooting hardware and apparel to be seen, and although the Sporting specialist will have hard and fast ideas as to the best gun and equipment needed to perform to maximum potential, virtually anything goes for those shooting Sporting for fun. A wide variety of guns will be used, from the most modern of competition over-and-under to the ancient side-by-side hammer gun, with all manner of permutations in between. Usually there will be no need for concern that you are not correctly equipped or dressed – as there may be at a more formal day – with the waxproof jacket as common as the purpose-made Skeet vest. Enjoyment is most definitely the name of the game.

COMPANY DAYS

The provision of clay-shooting facilities for corporate or company days is a fast-growing modern feature of the sport. Many larger companies treat their employees, contractors, consultants and the like to a day out, both as a reward for past endeavours and as an incentive for the future. Such days take various forms, golf being a widely used and traditional way of becoming better acquainted in the less stressful surroundings of the open air. Indeed, many a deal is struck at such venues, any cost incurred by the company proving a thoroughly worthwhile investment. Increasingly popular is the company clay-pigeon day, a valuable perk for those fortunate enough to receive an invitation.

The benefits to the sport from this type of activity are twofold. Firstly, and most obviously, there is the financial gain, which can be quite considerable in terms of comparisons with normal clay-shooting days. Secondly, there is the fact that here again the sport is being brought to the attention of a group of people who are often complete novices. All the comments made above about the have-a-go stand hold good except for the lack of cost to the individual.

Dependent on the size of the party of Guns involved, individual tuition may have a higher profile, with less interest in shooting a *bona fide* layout which may be comparable to that widely on offer at other clay-shooting events. The accent will usually be firmly on a light-hearted day out, although some form of prize may be offered by the company. The day will include refreshments, with a lengthy break for lunch, and the shoot organiser must be certain that all targets are compatible with the inevitably modest skills of most of the party.

STARSHOT

Few clay-shooting disciplines can be described as fun pure and simple. Most have both a serious and a less serious side. During the mid 1980s, in response to a search for a type of clay shooting which

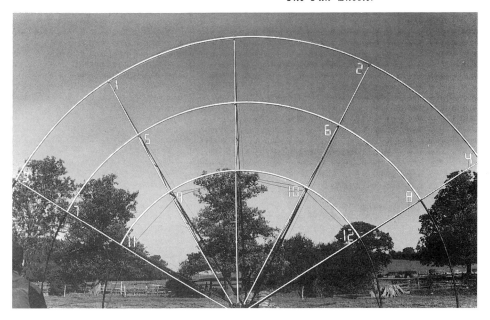

would be attractive as a spectator sport – especially for the lucrative medium of television – Starshot arrived on the scene. For a year or two it did receive widespread television exposure, principally because of its pro/celebrity format. The involvement of big-name stars, such as Ian Botham and Jackie Stewart, coupled with top shooting men such as A.J. Smith, created much interest. The event pitted men in pairs one against the other across the startlingly visual Starshot layout; it was good spectator stuff, and perhaps good television. Sadly, despite a heavy sell and a good deal of financial input, Starshot seems to have died a TV death; in this the negative effects of the Hungerford tragedy may well have had a more far-reaching influence than anyone thought at the time.

On the clay-shooting circuit itself, Starshot has never really taken off. Starshot layouts are inordinately expensive to install, and so not cheap to take part in; entry costs may be as much as 100 per cent above those for other disciplines, and it does not take a genius to understand that unless the product on offer is very special indeed, the paying public will soon give the thumbs down. Once the novelty value of Starshot wore off there appeared to be little to retain the shooter's interest. Indeed, the shooting itself could scarcely be considered a true test of skill, rather the development of a certain technique. The sort of ability necessary for success at Starshot is widely considered in clay-shooting circles as trick shooting, and as such has never created the sort of excitement and following that the inventors doubtless hoped for. Starshot is certainly fun, but will surely never satisfy the aspirations of those who seek sterner stuff.

6 Competition

The web of competitive shooting in Great Britain today is far-reaching and complex. A good deal of this sport has no other basis than the not inconsiderable enjoyment of winning a modest trophy or prize. But bigger prizes and sponsorship inevitably make competition more intense, paving the way for a new breed of near professional. Pressure becomes more intense when shooters begin to compete for the highest honours in the sport – the national and international championships, and the right to represent their country in world, Commonwealth and Olympic competition. We have all seen photographs of medal-festooned competitors returning happily from some great victory, but probably seldom stopped to think of the years of hard graft and sheer dedication, combined with a special talent, that have been vital precursors of the eventual triumph. It is a very special story and part of the whole complex clay-pigeon shooting scenario.

Although the days are gone when wealthy gentlemen wagered often fabulous sums – the most extreme examples took place on the Continent – competitions for large amounts of money do still occur. However, such sums are more likely to be made available by means of a modest contribution to an overall prize pool rather than by the individual placing of four-figure bets. If there is a throwback to the old big-money wagering days it must surely be in ZZ target shooting, and of course large sums also come from big business concerns, who increasingly wish to be associated with this boom sport through sponsorship.

For many shooters competition *per se* is a horrific concept which flies directly in the face of the proud shooting ethic which has been so painstakingly built up in Britain over hundreds of years. For them there is something vaguely obscene about any association between sport and the professionalism of competing for material reward; such a view is perhaps born of the British attitude that to compete is enough. The attitude of the clay shooter in the 1990s is somewhat more liberated, and is therefore probably a truer reflection of the modern world in which people work hard and play hard and where competition is the name of the game.

In essence there are three types of competitive clay shooting:

(a) The private affair organised within clubs or groups of friends and associates; these will be very much low-key, with prizes to match, and will very often be carried on in a relaxed and cordial atmosphere notwithstanding the extra edge enjoyed by those likely to turn in a good score.

(b) The Open shoot, which is – as the name implies – open to all-comers irrespective of status, and will include a vast array of shoots, all of which enjoy the common denominator of being outside the auspices of the CPSA.

(c) The Registered competition, which is governed by CPSA or UIT (International Shooting Union) Rules and Regulations and which now undoubtedly forms the basis of all serious competition. Most certainly, anyone who harbours any ambitions on the representative front – from basic county team level right through to the highest level of shooting for Great Britain – will be obliged to shoot Registered targets and will thus have to accept both the obligations and the benefits arising therefrom.

THE PRIVATE SHOOT

Throughout Britain there is an almost infinite number of shooting groupings, the vast majority of whom take part in clay shooting at some time or other in some form. Whether these are live quarry or target orientated, it is common for many of the constituent members to compete for some sort of prize some time during the year, even if it is only once a year to determine a local champion of sorts. Festival shoots are commonplace, at Christmas or Easter for example, with seasonal fare often on offer; the Turkey Shoot is frequently held and many a Christmas dinner has been provided by virtue of shooting prowess (the turkeys are dead before the shoot!). More commonly, trophies will be on offer, and some very attractive prizes are available at surprisingly low cost. Here it is very much horses for courses. The private shoot is not in the business of making the participant rich or of encouraging ill-feeling to creep in by offering fabulous rewards for a few hours' sport. However, there can be no denying that the vast majority of today's top shooters cut their shooting teeth in such an environment, so these types of shoot do perform a great service for the sport in a wider context.

THE OPEN SHOOT

Progression from the private shoot to the Open shoot is a natural one for many clay shooters. It is the most common route taken by emergent competitors as they make their way into the sport. As with many low-key events, the Open shoot can be anything the organisers desire, although the vast majority conform to the sort of English Sporting format outlined in Chapter 8. English Sporting is immensely popular and, although very labour intensive, it is fairly easy and cheap to set up, the main requirements being plenty of time and energy on the part of the organisers. Strictly speaking, Open shoots will not be run under the auspices of the CPSA, but be open to everyone, CPSA members and non-members alike. However, not infrequently the larger shoots do conform to CPSA rules and guidelines. The latter are based upon the sort of common sense needed to run a shoot effectively, while CPSA rules governing English Sporting take account of what is fair, practical and above all safe in this clay-shooting format. It is only the imprudent who do not seriously consider incorporating most of these facets in their Open shoot. There is a limited number of ways in which a shoot can be run, and to conform to tried and trusted methods is obviously eminently sensible for all concerned.

Entries at Open shoots can vary enormously. Where a shooting ground has a regular established following the number of competitors can run into the hundreds. At the sort of Open shoot invariably run in conjunction with a country fair or the Country Land Owners' (CLA) Game Fair, entries may be near to or in excess of a thousand, which gives an idea of just how popular English Sporting is. The number of entries are influenced by several factors: the basic format of the shoot; the track record of the ground and/or organisers; and the type and extent of the prizes on offer. This latter point may be crucial and there are accepted and expected parameters within which organisers usually work, these in turn being influenced by the actual size of the shoot – i.e., the number of targets (birds) on offer. English Sporting shoots are mostly in the forty or fifty bird bracket, while for such a massively attended event as the CLA Game Fair, expect thirty birds: this will be because of the need to process large numbers of entrants in the day without excessive delay and queueing. In addition there will always be a fair scattering of larger shoots – up to a maximum of a hundred birds. The number of targets on offer will give some indication of the type of shoot likely to be encountered, the shoot offering seventy-five to a hundred birds invariably being aimed at the ultra-serious competitively minded shooter. Here, the prizes are likely to be more substantial, and this will be reflected in the entry fee, which must foot the bill for the expense involved in setting up and running the shoot together with clays, prize monies and a profit for the organisers. For a hundred birds expect an entry fee (in 1991) to be over £20, although payout will often be £100 plus to the High Gun alone, with a good share of money further down the order.

Many of the smaller shoots offer a choice of trophies or cash by way of prizes; this is done for various reasons and is a tactic which really works, as is evident by the popularity of such events. Open shoots are

the main hunting ground for the somewhat predatory 'pot-hunter', a term rather unfairly ascribed to the clique of shooters of above-average ability who travel their locality every weekend in search of competition and prizes. In such cases substantial cash or other valuable prizes are the main target, and where these are on offer the clique may be quite a large group. In terms of ability the average shooter just cannot compete with this on a consistent basis and good prizes may act as a positive deterrent to the run-of-the-mill shooters who form the majority of those working the clay-pigeon circuit. However, as most top shooters usually have no interest in trophy prizes, the option 'cash or trophy' can offer the best of both worlds and is therefore universally popular. It is good to see such a prize format available, enabling good and less good shooters to operate within the same environment without one element feeling inhibited by the overpowering ability of the better Shots, or the other being aggravated by the presence of those with lesser ability.

Fabulous array of trophies at the British Open Skeet Championship, Kingsferry Gun Club

Any resentment directed towards top shooters who persist in using their considerable talents in the pursuit of prizes is, I feel, unfair, for they pay their entry fee at shoots throughout the land and, indeed, are a major factor in sustaining shoots through the inclement months of the year when the trophy hunter is more likely to be engaged in shooting fur and feather. This 'pot-hunting' class of shooter is undoubtedly among that group which might be considered 'near-professional', but they really do have a vital role to play in the maintenance of the sport on

45

an annual basis; their presence is not only acceptable but desirable. The only fly in the ointment is that some of them are not exactly renowned for good manners, diplomacy and humility. Most clay shooters are thoroughly nice people but, as in all sports, there is a tiny minority who give the sport a bad name by their inconsiderate and boorish behaviour. Sadly it is all too easy for all 'pot-hunters' to be branded the same.

The Open shoot can provide good fun and entertainment for a substantial band of clay shooters, both serious and less serious. As well as the main shoot it is common to find additional offerings, with a Pool shoot (usually a testing form of English Sporting over ten birds) often immensely popular. So, too, will be the practice and tuition stand, a valuable means of introducing aspiring shooters into the ways of clay shooting and the rudiments of handling a shotgun.

Thus the Open shoot can provide a tangible return to suit the needs of the individual competitor; it can be a first rung on the ladder for the newcomer to the sport; and it can serve as the next stepping stone for the shooter on his way towards the totally different world of CPSA competition and possibly ultimate national and international recognition.

THE REGISTERED SHOOT

Those shoots advertised as being 'Registered' are CPSA-registered and encompass all serious competitive shoots other than the sort of Open events referred to above. Most magazine-advertised fixtures lists are headed 'CPSA Fixtures' or something similar, and among the chronological listings such legends as '100 DTL reg.' denote the type and extent of competition. On any one weekend, usually on Sundays, dozens of Registered shoots take place up and down the country, offering a fair spread of disciplines. Registered shoots are for CPSA members only. Because a shooter's performance at Registered shoots is the crucial factor in determining selection for the various representative honours, it follows that only CPSA members can qualify to shoot for their country – or indeed for Great Britain. The CPSA is for shooters in England, with the other home countries – Wales, Scotland and Ireland – having their own clay-target governing associations, which form the basis for inter-country tournaments.

Throughout the various disciplines, no matter how diverse, there are certain central governing principles. Most notable among these for the shooter who graduates from the Open circuit is the classification system, which in essence turns each competition into a number of sub-competitions as shooters of differing ability battle it out for the class prizes. Each competition comprises four main classes, while large competitions provide additional classes encompassing Ladies, Colts,

Veterans, etc. For the domestic disciplines – that is, those governed by CPSA rules – of English Skeet, English Sporting and Down-the-Line together with its sub-divisions, there are classes in A/A, A, B and C; for the international disciplines – governed by UIT rules – of ISU Skeet, Automatic Ball Trap, Olympic Trap and Universal Trench there are classes in A, B, C and D; while for FITASC Sporting there are classes A, B and C. The qualifying percentages for each class (itemised in later chapters) vary enormously from one discipline to another. By way of example, in DTL the qualifying percentage for class A/A is 95 plus, while for the more demanding disciplines of FITASC Sporting the qualifying percentage for class A is 75 plus.

Prize monies at Registered shoots are usually self-generating from the entry fees paid by competitors, except where major sponsorship deals for the larger championship shoots apply, in which case they may be significantly higher. These in turn will be paid back in various ways. Most commonly there will be a certain amount set aside for the eventual overall winner – the High Gun – with the remainder divided among the classes. Some shoots pay out the same amount in each class, while others pay back class prize money according to entries. Either system of payback can cause disparities, as seldom are the entries evenly spread among the classes. Yet so long as the system used is seen to be fair there will seldom be complaints. Payback is at the discretion of the shoot organisers, the CPSA's only ruling being that the amount to be paid back is clearly displayed before the shoot starts; in this way the shooter knows the situation from the outset, and can decide whether it is worth his while entering. One thing is undeniable: no shooter will ever get rich from shooting at Registered events; sponsorship to a high level augmented by regular wins will be necessary before the shooter can hope even to cover his costs.

Nothing more readily causes grumbles and dissent on the Registered shoot circuit than the classification system. Over the years it has been the subject of complaint and disharmony, and although the CPSA, to its credit, is currently trying to trim the system into a better working framework, the fact remains that it is a system which is wide open to abuse. The term 'sandbagging' is widely used to describe those shooters who are suspected of shooting below their true form in order to attain a lower classification rating, and there can be no denying that this does occur. For me, this is cheating pure and simple and is a serious stigma within the sport. It may never be possible to determine just who is cheating and who is not (almost without doubt the CPSA would take firm disciplinary action against any member found to be so cheating), and it is something we shall have to live with. Even so, there is a variety of ploys which can be used at least to limit this reprehensible practice. No doubt in the fullness of time the regulating bodies will get round to implementing some of them.

Determining of members' averages is carried out in the following way: at present the qualification period is from 1 November in any given year until 31 October in the following year; any scores recorded at Registered shoots during that period will qualify for inclusion in the next edition of the Members' Averages and once an average is obtained this will stand for a full year. If the shooter continues to shoot Registered targets during the period for which his average stands, then a new average will appear in the next Averages book. If for any reason he does not shoot any Registered targets during the period for which he has obtained an average, his name will drop out of the book for the following year. In other words, it takes a full season, as defined above, to obtain an average, and if an average is to be maintained, the shooter must shoot Registered scores year in and year out. The minimum qualifying total is a hundred targets. Before 1989/90 all scores submitted to the CPSA by each shooter counted towards the next year's averages; thus a shooter could calculate with a degree of precision just what his recorded percentage would be, and from that in exactly which class he would be shooting for the coming year. This has been one of the main factors enabling unscrupulous shooters to manipulate their scores. In the opinion of many shooters the low qualifying number of a hundred targets – in effect one Registered shoot, as few Registered shoots these days will be over less than a hundred targets – has been one of the aids to cheating. This is not to say that all shooters turning in a score over only a hundred targets cheat – far from it – but this ruling does undoubtedly make it easier for a shooter to return an unrepresentative picture of true shooting ability. For the 1990/91 season the CPSA introduced a system whereby it is impossible for any shooter to work out their average, as not all returned scores will be allowed to stand for inclusion in making up the member's average for the forthcoming year; this will be achieved by computer cut-off, although nobody seems very certain as to how it will work. It will be interesting to see the outcome of this exercise when the new Averages book is printed and distributed.

For those shooters without a recorded entry in the Members' Averages book, the following procedures apply. No personal recorded average will exist; therefore each shooter will have to be classified on the day, and such a classification will last for that shoot only. For the domestic disciplines the scores achieved over the first half of the competition will determine the class for the day: for a fifty-target competition the first twenty-five targets; for a hundred-target competition the first fifty targets; for a seventy-five target competition, again the first fifty targets. Thus for DTL, for example, a score of 95 per cent or over (143/150 or more) will result in an A/A classification; were the shooter to repeat this feat over his second fifty targets he would record 286/300, which would be a reasonable score by any standards but one which would be very unlikely to put him into the prize money. Shooting as an unclassified shooter in Registered competitions can be a heart-breaking and dispiriting experience: if you shoot your first fifty badly enough to achieve a class C rating (under 85 per cent, or 127/150 or below) then you have almost certainly blown any chance of winning a class C prize; while if you shoot well enough to get into class A/A you will need to hit virtually everything to have any chance at all. For the non-domestic disciplines the draw system applies: 'For a 100 bird shoot a draw will take place *after* 75 targets have been shot – on the completion of stage three. Two numbers will be drawn at random from one to three and these two numbers will decide the two stages to count for the classification of unclassified shooters in the event.'

Once a shooter is into the system the situation becomes stabilised and it is often possible to win the occasional class prize. Despite earlier comments about cheating, it must be clearly acknowledged that the vast majority of shooters are decent and honest competitors who want nothing more than to improve their own standard and, if possible, to pick up the occasional prize en route; for most CPSA members the likelihood of winning national or international honours is remote, but they enjoy their sport just the same. The absence of this large nucleus of what are essentially non-winners would make clay shooting a very poor spectacle indeed, and the winners would find their returns substantially slashed. Without a large, keen following the growth of the sport would come to a grinding halt. Those who aspire to the highest levels would do well to remember just who it is who pays for the constant regeneration of the sport on an annual basis.

Competitive clay shooting can be a wonderful stimulant to those who take part, irrespective of the level at which it is carried out. Whether the ultimate reward is the most modest of trophies at the local farmers' shoot or the gold medal at the Olympic Games, the achievement in winning remains relative to the person's commitment and ability. Competition is one of the major reasons why clay shooting exists in Britain in its present form, and long may this situation prevail.

7 *The Governing Bodies*

To all intents and purposes clay shooting in Britain is governed by the Clay Pigeon Shooting Association. To a lesser extent the Home Country Associations in Scotland, Wales and Ireland govern sport in their regions, but it is the CPSA which really gets down to the nitty-gritty of organising the large championships, running all Registered competitions via its regional network and steering all clay shooters along the correct road as far as training and safety are concerned. Founded in 1928 as the successor to the British Trap Shooting Association, the CPSA struggled on for many years with a small membership which belied its considerable influence on and responsibility for the sport, until the more rapid growth of the late 1980s. The number of people shooting clays in some form or other is almost impossible to ascertain, but it could easily be anything up to 200,000; there is therefore an enormous reservoir of potential members for the CPSA to tap into. Even if the present actual membership figure seems relatively low at around 29,000 (late 1990), this figure does compare favourably with other years and there is a demonstrable and continuing growth. In fact there can never be a membership figure which in any way reflects the number of people shooting clays, most CPSA members being the serious competition shooters; yet the membership package is a good one, and does much to encourage the less ambitious clay shooter to join in order to take advantage of the £1,000,000 insurance cover and the excellent monthly members' magazine.

Clay shooting in this country has seen some rather lack-lustre organisation over the years, but since the CPSA gained a firmer grip on the sport by virtue of its expanding membership things have improved out of all recognition. With this expansion has come the need gradually to reorganise, with the devolvement of power away from the Executive and full-time officials in favour of first regional, and latterly county, committees being undoubtedly a positive step. Now local shoots and championships will be run by the county or region responsible for the area concerned, and with direct elections from the membership to the county committees there can be no sustainable charge that such committees are unrepresentative.

Facilities on offer in a region are undoubtedly restricted to some extent by the amount of monies coming in, and it should therefore follow that the regions with the largest number of members are the more active and energetic. This is unfortunately not always the case, but nevertheless a breakdown is interesting inasmuch as it gives an insight into the membership bias. Figures for 1989 show that the South East is by far the largest region with 38.36 per cent of the total CPSA membership and 34.16 per cent of CPSA affiliated clubs. But the South East is very much a one-off region. The other English regions are remarkably similar in make-up one to another: West Midlands 15.20 per cent (14.72 per cent); South West 14.99 per cent (15.27 per cent); North 13.99 per cent (15.13 per cent); East Midlands 13.57 per cent (13.05 per cent), and Scotland, Wales, etc. 3.8 per cent (7.6 per cent). The CPSA policy of administration at local level works well. The more mundane matters such as ground registrations and inspections can be carried out by local honorary representatives rather than tying down full-time officers in time-consuming site visits. Crucially, the headquarters staff are there as a back-up when needed. The provision of adequate facilities is one of the biggest challenges facing any ruling body; the CPSA tackles this issue by the maintenance of strict criteria for its affiliated clubs, and it is these criteria which ensure a continuity of standards throughout the country. Thus we can be assured that the specification of layouts and regulation of targets remain a constant – as indeed they must do if shooting abilities are to be enhanced. Of great importance, safety aspects at grounds are given close and on-going attention, and only those clubs which maintain a high safety standard may continue to run Registered shoots.

International competitions such as the Olympic disciplines of Olympic Trap and ISU Skeet are administered by the UIT or ISU. Additionally, much European competition for Universal Trench, ZZ and FITASC Sporting will be governed by FITASC. At home the CPSA still records all scores at Registered shoots, but the affairs relating to such disciplines are governed by the International Board rather than the CPSA at headquarters. The British International Board (BIB) is a virtually autonomous adjunct of the CPSA; it rules the international disciplines, taking responsibility for all related matters including qualification for national and international honours.

Money is always a problem in the clay-shooting world. It is a difficulty which besets the BIB as it struggles to help finance the efforts of Great Britain's top shooters. A projected national shooting ground, which would play host to all the major championships and would be run by the sport for the sport, has been a long-standing dream but again lack of finance is a major stumbling block for the CPSA.

8 English Sporting

The origins of English Sporting as a competitive discipline go back many years, the first Sporting Championship having been held in 1925. In the competitive field its popularity seems to know no bounds. Indeed, the larger events are frequently over-subscribed. One possible explanation for its huge popularity is the wide variety of targets on offer at any big event. Love it or loathe it, there can be no denying that English Sporting is by far the most wide-ranging, demanding and challenging of all domestic disciplines. This is supported by a cursory glance at the qualifying averages for the various classes, which show that to achieve A/A classification (the highest class) the shooter will need to break 75 per cent plus of targets as opposed to 94 per cent plus for English Skeet and 95 per cent plus for Down-the-Line.

There is a great deal more to tackling English Sporting than simply shooting in the competitive CPSA-regulated manner. As outlined in Chapter 5, the casual shooters who make up the vast majority of clay shooters overall shoot English Sporting almost exclusively, mostly outside the influence of the CPSA. Undoubtedly a fair proportion of such casuals do not see their chosen pastime as English Sporting; to them it is Sporting pure and simple, and they have no great interest in any other form of clay shooting. It would be no exaggeration to say that many of them do not even know of the existence of such things as Automatic Ball Trap and the Trench disciplines, and if they do they do not care a great deal. Almost certainly it is fair to say that CPSA-Registered shoots are anathema to many such shooters. They prefer to enjoy their sport in a rather more low-key manner without any of the ultra-competitive element or the pressures inherent in sticking rigidly to rules and regulations. Many people prefer the small *ad hoc* shoot, which is not to say that such shoots are run in an indisciplined fashion. On the contrary, many of the conventions surrounding the workings of the larger shoots are present further down the scale, simply because they are based on sound common sense.

This chapter is intended to create a fair picture of all the complexities which go to make a day at an English Sporting event. Whether the shoot is small or large, the parameters are broadly the same, and because of this I use Registered competition as my datum;

where rigid criteria exist these will be cited, indeed recommended – if all shoots conformed to such criteria there would unquestionably be many all-round benefits. Safety is obviously at the top of the list of considerations at any shoot. English Sporting is at least as potentially dangerous as any other discipline – if not more so; because of widespread individual stands, the shoot organisers must take account of the positioning of each stand in relation to another, and of course be particularly aware of the inherent dangers occasioned by the fall of shot. For the larger shoots (a hundred targets for example) plenty of room is advisable, although some fairly compact grounds do exist and this need not detract from the enjoyment of the shoot or create extra safety hazards. In fact, it is surprising to find just how close individual stands can be without interfering with one another.

Waiting to shoot

So long as certain criteria are taken into account, a Sporting layout can be anything the organisers wish it to be, and it is very unlikely that two shooting grounds will offer precisely the same layout, apart from inevitable similarities in format. The organiser will usually seek to provide both an enjoyable course and one which will test the best of Shots in a fair manner; he may set the targets in any fashion, provided that Rule 8 is complied with: 'At each stand, the trajectories shall be the same for each shooter in height, distance and speed. It must be possible for all targets to be hit within the effective range of a 12-bore shotgun ... these trajectories, established and calculated in calm weather, may be altered by wind, but if so altered, will remain regular targets.' The organiser may use any type or combination of targets, providing that no more than 30 per cent of such targets are non-standard (non-standard will include mini, midi, battue, rocket and rabbit clays – also referred to by some as FITASC targets, see Chapter 9). A variety of colours may be offered, black and orange being the most common. Actual target combinations vary somewhat, the organiser occasionally offering single targets. But in the main the stands will consist of pairs of targets which will be defined as follows:

(a) A report pair – a pair where the second target is launched at the sound of the gun firing at the first target.

(b) A following pair – a pair where the second target is launched as soon and as safely as possible after the first target from the same trap.

(c) A simultaneous pair – a pair where both targets are launched simultaneously, either from the same trap or from two different traps.

Thus English Sporting is simplicity itself in concept, though like most concepts it is somewhat different in practice.

Tradition decrees that Sporting targets should attempt to emulate the flight of some creature in the wild – an impossibility, of course, in the strictest sense, although the shooter will know what to expect on each shooting stand where the target type is named. For example, if the term 'Driven' is used – such as 'Driven Partridge' – then the shooter knows he will have to deal with some sort of in-coming target, in the case of the Partridge a low one. Today stand titles are perhaps not that important, as shooters know full well that they are competing against artificial targets. However, stand titles do ensure the retention of that traditional air which is part and parcel of Sporting clays.

The non-standard target is an important tool for the organiser wishing to put on an interesting and varied course; yet even where there is 100 per cent use of standard clays variety can still be guaranteed – so long as the will to create it is there. It is the non-regulation of Sporting layout specifications that establishes this discipline as the most difficult available; the most apparently in-significant alteration either at the trap or on the shooting stand can make the target appear radically different from one presented, say, the week before, and it speaks volumes for the intricacies of Sporting that many fine Shots are defeated by the subterfuges of angle and speed rather than by sheer distance and blinding velocity.

Target-for-target Sporting can be as difficult as any of the disciplines described later in this book, and but for the constant practice at repetitious targets (the term 'repetitious' is not meant to be in any way derogatory) then scores at, say, English Skeet would be far lower than they actually are. With Sporting, of course, it is not possible to practise at targets with any certainty that they will be presented in that form on any given shoot on any given day. However, practice at any type of target will be better than no practice at all, and will enable the Sporting shooter to develop his ability to 'read' the flight of each target. Notwithstanding the fact that targets will vary greatly from one shoot to another, it is possible to practise on certain target types, something which is especially relevant if the shooter has a particular weakness. Once he has achieved familiarity with a target type, he will be well able to tackle the variations to be encountered in competition, even if he does not become inch-perfect on every variation.

EQUIPMENT

Traps

The beauty and ease of Sporting is that literally any trap will do to launch a clay. In extreme cases it is not unknown for rabbit targets to be rolled manually down a sloping trackway to offer a slow and deceptively difficult target, there being no trap at all. Traps can vary enormously from the most simple single arm, through more complex

Magazine trap

types allowing variations in speed, height and angle, to the most sophisticated fully automatic magazine-fed trap on the market. All throw variously challenging targets, and it is a foolish shooter who dismisses a target simply because it is launched from a slow old trap.

Guns and ammunition

Broadly speaking, any gun will suffice. An average field-grade weapon will do, and so long as it possesses a middle-of-the-road type of choking (such as $\frac{1}{4}$ and $\frac{1}{2}$) then the user will be under no handicap. Nevertheless, users of some amazingly unsuitable weapons often return phenomenally good scores in spite of – rather than because of – their weaponry. However, the expert Sporting shooter will probably use one of the new generation of Sporting or Sporter weapons, often with the multi-choke facility. These mostly have long barrels – 30-inch or even 32-inch are now commonplace – together with changeable choke tubes, although many top shooters still use fixed chokes. Trap guns are also favoured by a number of people, but in all probability with some of the choke removed; many Sporting shooters prefer a gun which shoots a trifle high – which the Trap gun most certainly does – in order that the target always remains clearly in view; yet what suits one shooter will not necessarily suit another. The semi-automatic is also a useful Sporting tool, although the single barrel and its inherent lack of choke flexibility on the doubles can be off-putting, the shooter often being forced to compromise; however, compromise is not necessarily a bad thing, and if it is necessary the shooter would be well advised to opt for a choke which errs on the open side rather than one that is over-tight.

The great majority of targets on offer can be comfortably broken with a fairly open choke. Choice of choke, where a choice exists, will obviously vary from shoot to shoot. The astute shooter will decide upon his weaponry after viewing the targets on offer. Walking an unknown Sporting layout in order to view the targets and perhaps to see how other shooters may be tackling individual stands is a thoroughly worthwhile exercise, and will repay the thoughtful shooter in terms of a few extra 'ticks' on his scorecard at the end of the day. It will also allow a little more time to consider the options available, and may make a big difference when it comes to tackling those extra-difficult targets which are often found somewhere or other on a large Sporting layout.

It is a not uncommon sight on the Sporting layout to come across the shooter carrying two guns. It may be because he possesses a weapon with no multi-choke facility, or perhaps a change of gun is advisable on certain stands. For example, where the long-range rising target is on offer the Trap gun may be the ideal choice; alternatively for the close-dropping target the Trap gun would prove a positive disadvantage,

while the field-grade or Sporting gun would come into its own. The shooter who can change from one gun to another without detriment to performance can find many inherent benefits throughout a layout, although under the rules he will not be permitted to change guns once he is actually on the shooting stand. On the other hand, the option of a change of gun, or a change of choke-tube, will not always be an advantage. Many relatively inexperienced shooters spend too much time fretting about their choice of choke rather than concentrating on what is required to break the target.

There is a great deal to be said for a compromise choice, while sticking to the same weapon is to be recommended for all but the most proficient of shooters.

Ammunition, too, will vary enormously. Many manufacturers offer specialist Sporting loads, and very effective most of them are; however, once again it will be for the shooter to decide in the light of experience – the targets again being the determining factor. Shot size is an important consideration: number 8 shot is a good all-round Sporting size, and will be more than capable of accounting for the great majority of targets. However, where a target is at longer range and edge on, so that its more vulnerable open face is protected, it may take a good-quality Trap load of 7½s combined with a tighter choke to guarantee a broken clay. Similarly, the harder clays such as rabbit and battue, especially if they are at a good range, may need that extra bit of killing power to ensure a break. For really close targets, such as the low driven, smaller number 9 shot will be just the job, with the dense pattern of small shot fired from an open choke more likely to make up for any deficiencies in the shooter's technique. Once again the shooter needs to be aware of the targets on offer before deciding on cartridge load and shot size. It is certainly possible for the shooter casually to approach a shoot with fixed choke and the same cartridges throughout, and to come in with a more than passable score; but it is when the competition is at its most fierce that the crucial difference between winning and losing may be determined by one chipped clay and by the choice of shot size. The variety of cartridge loads and types on offer can have an effect on the choke itself. Without going into unnecessary technicalities, it is worth recording that a cup wad will tighten the spread of shot, while a felt wad is likely to enhance spread. There are many options open to the Sporting shooter, although in the formative years it will not be helpful to fret too much about chokes and loads. In terms of other accessories the Sporting shooter needs above all else a good strong bag of some sort, especially where he may need to carry over a hundred cartridges, possibly of different types, around a widely spread course; the bag should be large enough to accommodate earmuffs, showerproof coat, gloves, etc.

THE RULES

The full rules governing English Sporting are contained in CPSA Booklet No. 10. The following extracts concern shooting, scoring and the shooter's conduct.

Rule 3/4

Guns must not exceed a calibre of 12 gauge.
Cartridges must not be loaded with more than 28 grammes (1 ounce). The shot shall be spherical shot of normal production lead, diameter between 2mm and 2.6mm, English sizes 6–9: plated shot may be used. Home loads may not be used. The Referee may at any time take an unfired cartridge out of a shooter's gun for examination. If the cartridge is found not to comply with the regulations, all targets on that particular stand will be counted as lost.

Rule 9 Target Killed

The target is killed when it has been launched and the shooter has shot it according to the rules, and at least one visible bit of it has broken off, or it has been totally or partially pulverised.

Rule 10 Target Missed

(a)   When it has not been hit.
(b)   If only dusted or deflected.
(c)   If the shooter is unable to fire because he has left the safety catch

on, has forgotten to load or cock, if the gun is insufficiently broken or closed or if the shooter has forgotten to take the necessary measures to load the chamber (when he uses a single barrel gun).

(d)   If it is the fourth or more malfunction of the gun or ammunition occurring at the same stand.

(e)   If the shooter is unable to fire his second shot, having not put in a second cartridge, or if he has cancelled the locking device of the loading chamber of an automatic weapon, or if the safety catch engages due to recoil of the first shot, or if the second cartridge is ejected by the recoil or opened and emptied by the recoil for any other reason.

(f)   If the second shot cannot be fired because a shooter using a single trigger gun has not released the trigger sufficiently having fired his first shot.

(g)   If the shooter in the case of a malfunction, opens it himself or touches the safety catch before the Referee has examined the gun.

(h)   If the shot is not fired for another reason which does not give right to another target.

(i)   If the shooter (without legitimate reason) does not shoot at a regular double.

(j)   If the shooter (without legitimate reason) does not shoot the second target of a regular double, the result of the first is scored, and the second is declared lost.

Rule 13 Viewing Point
Any shooter who has not had an opportunity to see targets on any stand . . . shall have the right to be shown it/them.

Rule 14 Shooting and Sighting
Shooting and sighting practice is not allowed . . .

Rule 16 Gun Malfunctions
The shooter shall be allowed three gun or ammunition malfunctions not attributable to him on each stand without being penalised. A fourth or later malfunction shall be counted as lost or pair lost.

In the case of jamming of the gun which in the Referee's opinion cannot be repaired on the spot without being the shooter's fault, the shooter will be allowed to fire with another gun if he can get one immediately. Otherwise he may shoot his remaining targets later but only with the Referee's permission.

In the case of misfiring or malfunction, the shooter has to remain where he is, the gun pointing down the range, not opened, and without touching the safety catch before the Referee has examined the gun.

Two cartridges can be used on each single target . . .

In the case of a gun or ammunition malfunction on a single target, provided the shooter has been able to fire one shot, the result shall be scored.

In the doubles the shooter has the right to shoot either of the targets first. Should the shooter kill both targets together with either the first or the second shot, the result will be scored pair killed.

In a double, the shooter having missed his first target may fire his second cartridge at the same target . . . the second target being counted as lost.

Rule 17 No Target

The clay will be 'No Target' and a new target will be launched, the shooter having fired or not, if:

(a)   The target is broken at the start.

(b)   The target is launched from the wrong trap.

(c)   Two targets are launched simultaneously when a single should have been thrown.

(d)   The target is definitely of another colour than the targets used for the competition at that stand.

(e)   The first or second target of a double is irregular.

(f)   Two targets are launched simultaneously during a report pair or a following pair.

(g)   The target is launched before the shooter has said 'ready'.

(h)   The target is launched after a delay of more than three seconds.

(i)   The target zigzags, or its initial speed is not sufficient, or its trajectory is irregular.

(j)   The shooter misses his first target and this target collides with the second before the shooter has fired his second shot.

In the case of a 'No Target' in any form of doubles the shooter will be asked to fire a second double to determine the scores of the two shots. This will also apply in the case of malfunction of gun or ammunition not attributable to the shooter, provided that it is not the fourth time on that stand.

The Referee may also order the launching of a new target when:

(a)   The shooter has been materially disturbed.

(b)   The Referee cannot decide for any reason if the target has been killed or lost.

The Referee cannot in any case give a 'No Target' if the shooter has missed for any reason other than those stated in the 'No Target' rules.

Various other provisions exist dealing with the duties of the Referee and those of the Jury, none of which need really concern the normal clay shooter, other than as under:

Rule 18 Referee's Duties
The Referee's decision can be brought to the attention of the Jury . . . insofar as this DOES NOT CONCERN LOST OR KILLED TARGETS OR IRREGULAR TARGETS, WHERE THE REFEREE'S DECISION IS FINAL.

Also under:

Rule 19 Jury
At every competition a jury of five shooters representative of the shooters present shall be appointed.

THE LAYOUT AND TECHNIQUE

As there are no standard layout specifications for English Sporting, I have selected a sample layout from a hundred-target event, which demonstrates the sort of variety to be encountered on the larger Sporting shoot. I am indebted to the proprietor of Southdown Sporting Gun Club, in West Sussex, for this splendid array of targets spread over fourteen shooting stands. It was very much a thinking Sporting shooter's layout, with a wide variety of target types, and subtle angles and speeds.

Stand 1: Crossing and quartering
These consisted of four pairs of standard black targets released by bell (by remote command to the trapper so that the shooter did not need to shout). The targets came from right to left at no great height; the crosser was a close 20-yard target, something which ought to present few problems to the experienced Shot, although the quartering target was edging away all the time and the shooter needed to be able to read the precise angle and judge the correct amount of left-hand side needed to take up the necessary amount of lead to achieve a break. A

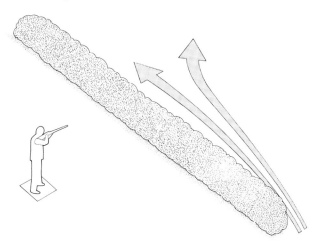

Figure 4 Crossing pair, with the outer target drifting away

relatively easy pair, with the closer target needing to be shot first and requiring small shot and open choke to maximise pattern; that quarterer was, however, the trickier shot of the pair and was probably at something approaching 40 yards by the time the shot was taken. As with all end-on targets, $7\frac{1}{2}$s and a tighter choke would have been the best bet.

Stand 2: Ducks to decoy

This offered four pairs of standard black clays moving from left to right released by bell. In typical decoying bird fashion the targets moved up to the shooter at less than 30 yards' range before beginning to dip as they lost velocity. The shooter was confronted by targets effectively moving in an arc, and was faced with the dilemma of shooting them early or late – either way the targets were never in level flight and although not difficult were certainly very deceptive. Unquestionably an opportunity to use smaller shot, such as 8s, while an open choke of about $\frac{1}{4}$ was ideal. It was necessary to lead the first target by a small amount as it levelled out, with the second requiring the shooter to drop his gun down through the target in order to take up lead and effect a kill.

Figure 5 Classic 'decoying duck' dropping pair

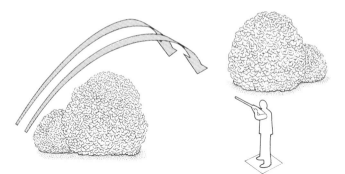

Stand 3: Grouse

Four pairs of standard clays, one black and the other blaze, released by bell. These flew level with the ground after being launched from out of range. A tricky pair of targets with the blaze edging nearer while the black moved progressively further away. The shooter who took the black first invariably found the blaze flashing past too rapidly for a successful shot, while any delay in firing as the targets passed found both clays losing velocity and both slowing and dipping. The optimum combination here was to take the blaze at about 20 yards as it crossed the shooter's front, with open choke and small shot, while the black needed larger shot and perhaps $\frac{1}{4}$ choke. A moderately difficult pair.

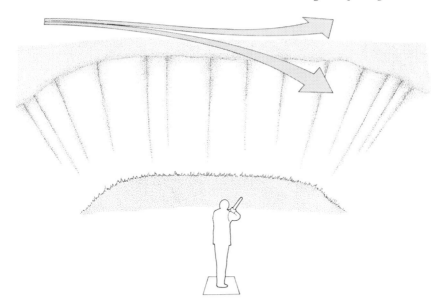

Stand 4: Teal

Four pairs of standard black clays released on the command of 'Pull'.
A typical teal target with the clays rising from close to the shooter's
left hand and moving obliquely across his front climbing rapidly all the
time. The left-hander fell away first and therefore needed breaking
first in order to allow the easier breaking of the second while it was still
climbing. No great range poser here, with neither target ever much
further away than about 30 yards; 8s and fairly open choke required,
but as with all teal targets it was vital not to delay too much if the targets
were to be shot either on the rise or at the peak of their climb.

Figure 6 Driven
grouse, with the
pair splitting as
they lose
momentum

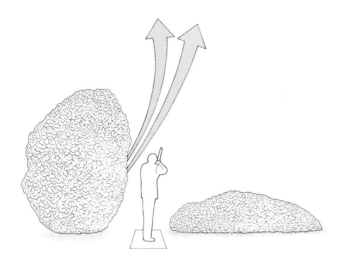

Figure 7 The teal
stand

Stand 5: Midi and standard

Four pairs as specified released on the command of 'Mark'. These
were launched from behind the shooter and passed close to the right
shoulder, being driven downwards off a slight rise in the ground,
making for a fast and testing pair. Here the shooter stood on a raised
platform some 10 feet off the ground overlooking a shallow valley, and
this tended to accentuate the dropping effect of the pair; the shooter
needed to fire below the dropping targets on both occasions, with the
second shot requiring a fair degree of drop. A testing pair, in terms of
both speed and range, with the range increasing rapidly the whole
while. A moderate amount of choke at least was needed for both shots,
with an almost end-on shot for the first target, and a couple of feet of
drop for the second as the target drove down into the vale.

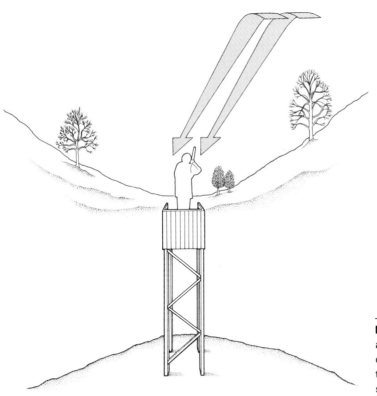

Figure 8 An awkward pair driven down past the shooter's right shoulder

Shooting from a raised platform

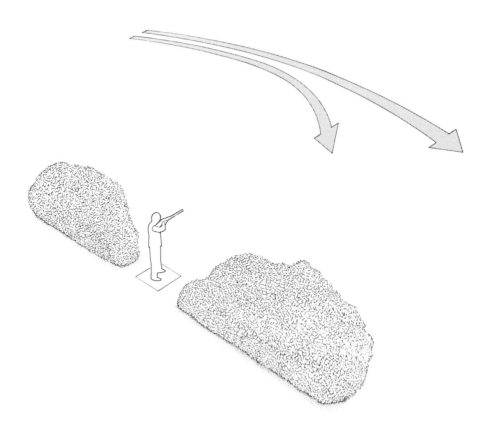

Stand 6: Battue and midi

Three pairs released by bell. These came from left to right, the midi in level flight moving fairly quickly, with the battue running out of velocity in front of the shooter. Neither target was further away than about 30 yards, although the battue turned on its side directly in front of the shooter's left-hand side and fell towards the ground as the velocity died. It was essential to take the battue first otherwise it would have been hopelessly lost as it dropped to the ground, while the midi was a straightforward crossing target. Unless he is very experienced, the shooter is inclined to become mesmerised by the battue, so it is essential to fire as soon as the target turns to show its vulnerable underside; in such a situation open choke and 8s would be ideal, with 8s again and a slightly tighter choke to deal with the midi.

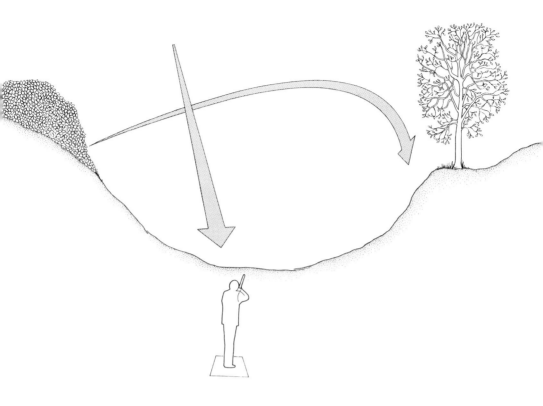

Stand 7: Battue and driven mini

Three report pairs released by bell. The battue came from left to right at about 30 yard's range and was much faster than it appeared; once again it turned on its side as the velocity failed and began to fall steeply. On report a mini was driven at moderate height to the shooter's left-hand side – a straightforward shot although moving very quickly. The battue was launched along the top of a bank so that the shooter needed to look up towards the treetops for the target; its velocity began to fail as it approached a large beech tree and this seemed to have the effect of lulling the shooter into believing that the battue was far slower than it actually was. Once again a moderate amount of choke and 8s fired as the target turned was likely to be ideal. The report mini came very quickly, as minis always do, from the top of the bank; open choke and 9s for a close fast target would have worked well.

Figure 10 A crossing battue followed by a fast driven mini

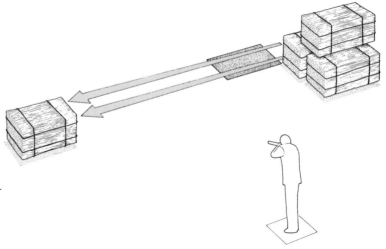

Figure 11 The rabbit stand. The targets must be broken between the bales

Rabbit track

Stand 8: Rabbits

Four pairs of targets released on the command of 'Pull'. These were released at about 30 yards' range and passed within 20 yards of the shooter, moving fairly slowly from right to left; however, the pair were also moving a little into the shooter, giving a slightly angled shot. The trick was to be sure to break both before they reached the 'shelter' of a strategically placed straw bale, the shooter being left with about 30 yards in which to break the pair. There ought to have been few problems for the shooter here, provided that he neither hung on the

There they go!

Pair killed!

pair and allowed them to run out of bounds, or got an unlucky bounce just at the moment of firing. Some rabbit tracks are notoriously bumpy, but this one was reasonably smooth, with the target running well from the rubber matting which was placed to minimise breakages at launch, of which there were remarkably few. Open choke and small shot were ideal here due to the closeness of the targets, but as with all ground or low-flying targets the shooter needed to hold the gun low in order to avoid shooting over the top. Open choke and 9s would be more than adequate at this sort of target.

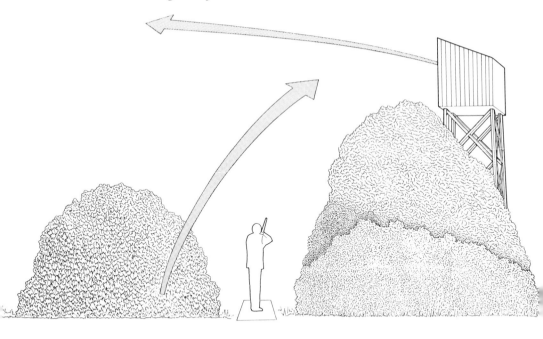

Figure 12 Crosser, with dropping curlew on report

Stand 9: Crosser with curlew

Three report pairs of standard black released by bell. A fast right-to-left crosser, at a good height after being released from a low 20-foot tower, flying across a gap in trees, with the 'curlew' a fast quartering-away target on report (curlew in West Sussex must be of a different species to the ones I am used to in Kent!). The crosser seemed deceptively slow but needed a careful measured swing and a big lead as it crossed at all of 40 yards out, while the curlew needed a determined amount of right-hand side and the tiniest amount of drop. In both cases a moderate amount of choke and either 8s or 7½s were needed. This was the classic report pair needing good timing to deal with one ostensibly slow target and one very fast and instant clay. A well-thought-out stand, of the type most shooters enjoy.

Stand 10: Crow

Four pairs of standard black in-comers released by bell. Here the shooter faced a trap hidden above him on a gentle slope; the targets were launched from about 60–70 yards away so that their flight took them over a tall tree. Thereafter they dropped tantalisingly towards the shooter, requiring the muzzles to be moved down through the target in order to take up the necessary lead. A fairly undemanding pair, but all too easy to underlead them and miss over the top. An open choke and 8s was the ideal combination here, but it was vital to keep the gun moving, for although the pair were slow moving they most certainly did not stop in mid-air, as many shooters found out to their cost.

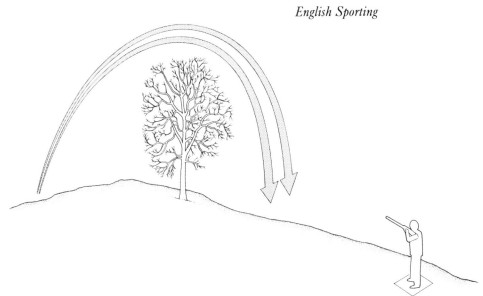

Figure 13 Dropping crow

Stand 11: Auto with blaze

Three report pairs of standard clays, one black and one blaze, released by bell. These consisted of a very fast and low black target quartering away from behind the shooter's left shoulder. A very deceptive target this, travelling not quite straight away at no more than head height. It required a small amount of right-hand side to achieve a break, while the shooter had to concentrate on keeping the gun moving in order to avoid being beaten by speed, at the same time making a conscious effort to keep the muzzles down. Following on was a very fast low orange target travelling from right to left and quartering slightly, little more than 4 feet off the ground. This latter target needed a small lead and some left-hand side, but as it was also dropping the shooter had to guard against shooting over the top. Ideally the auto target was best tackled using a degree of choke (about ½ choke would have been ideal) and 7½s, while the report target could be broken easily enough with open choking and 8s.

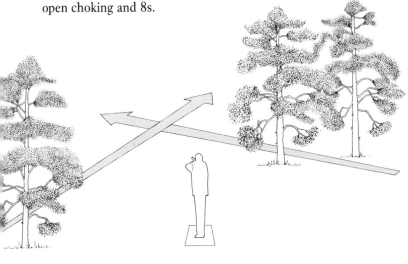

Figure 14 Low fast pair, with the right-hand target on report

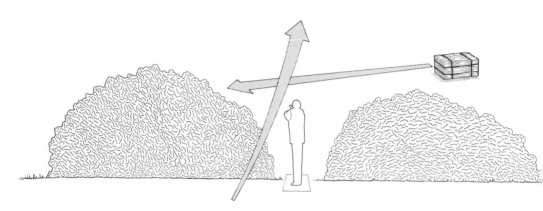

Figure 15 Rabbit, with fast going away target on report

Stand 12: Fur and feather

Three report pairs consisting of a rabbit with a midi on report, released on the command of 'Pull'. Here was a very close rabbit released from right to left, followed by a fast quartering-away midi released from behind the shooter's left shoulder. A fairly straightforward pair this, but still needing the utmost care to achieve maximum success. The rabbit was easy enough so long as the shooter kept the muzzle well down in order to guard against shooting over the top, while a small lead was all that was needed. The midi was not a difficult target either, needing plenty of right-hand side and a fast swing in order to guard against being caught out by the speed. The most interesting facet here was the contrast between very slow and very fast targets. Choke/shot combination would be open choke and 9s for the rabbit, with moderate choke and either 8s or 7½s for the report target.

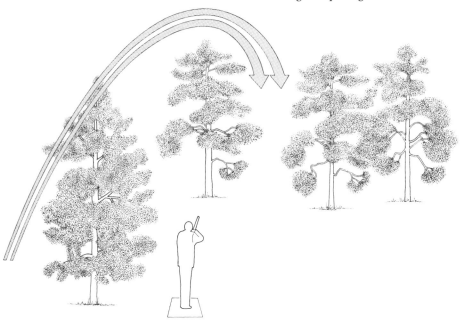

Stand 13: Curlew

Four pairs of standard black clays released on the command 'Mark'. These were released from the shooter's left-hand side and passed away quartering through a gap in the trees. Clever siting of the trap, with the base at an angle so that the trap was canted to one side, ensured that the targets did not fly true but dipped wickedly in the manner of the battue. Plenty of speed too, so that unless the shooter was exceptionally quick he was obliged to take the shots at dropping targets. The shooter could get away with a minimal lead below on the first target, but a huge lead below the dropping target was necessary on the second. Something like $1/4$ choke and 8s would have proved an ideal combination here. Not easy.

Figure 16 The sharply dropping targets on the curlew stand

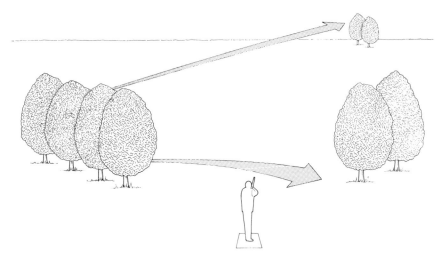

Stand 14: Crosser and midi

Three report pairs consisting of a very long-range standard, followed by a close fast midi on report. The first target was undoubtedly one of the most testing of the entire shoot. Crossing at something approaching 50 yards from left to right and travelling deceptively slowly, it required a huge lead for a break. The report bird was very close and fast from left to right, passing as close as 10 yards; it required an instinctive reaction, and a rapid swing and shot were necessary if a hit was to result – even then it was likely to outpace the shooter unless he was very alert. Ideally the shooter would be well advised to use at least ½ choke and 7½s on the long crosser, with open choke and 9s for the report target.

It says a great deal for the skill of the modern-day Sporting shooter that after this very varied and challenging shoot two scores of 94 were posted, although in general a score above 85 was considered good. The variety of targets, in both distribution and type, was as good as could be found anywhere and it is worth while commenting on one of the hidden factors which is often overlooked by the ordinary shooter – cost. The competition entry fee was £22, a little higher than the norm perhaps; however, the cost of staging such a varied shoot is high, with many report targets and the liberal use of the more expensive rabbit, battue, midi, mini and blaze targets. The expense involved in putting on a fourteen-stand shoot of such variety is immense, and this is highlighted by the fact that the organiser needed 120 entries just to break even. It is worth considering the inherent cost of running Sporting shoots, with even the more modest forty or fifty target event being far more labour intensive and therefore costlier than, say, a comparable Skeet or DTL shoot. For the future the way ahead must be for Sporting shoots to be run with fully automated layouts (on the shoot described above there were three automatic traps). Such traps remove the variable element of the human trapper (at some shoots, where inexperienced trappers are involved, this can be a major problem), with the automatic trap invariably throwing wonderfully consistent targets. Nor will there be variation from one trapper to another, as can sometimes occur with manually operated traps; while for the shoot organiser there will be none of the problems and expense of finding trappers on a regular basis. On the debit side there will be the initial capital cost (automatic traps cost about £3000 each at 1990 prices), although this cost will gradually be recouped by the savings in trapper costs; in addition there is the relative problem of moving and siting traps which are always heavy and unwieldy, while occasional breakdowns can be aggravating. However, on balance the automated Sporting layout is greatly to be favoured, and as the larger grounds change over, shooters can look forward to better and more consistent targets on a regular basis.

HIGH STANDARDS

Defining what is good shooting varies significantly from one discipline to another. The averages for defining classes are as good a guide as any, with the relatively low average of 75 per cent or over needed to achieve a top rating (class A/A) in English Sporting. Thus, anyone regularly shooting 85 per cent plus is shooting remarkably well. Despite the widespread availability of English Sporting, reference to the CPSA Members' Averages book shows that although it is by far the most widely popular discipline in Britain today, it is shot on a regular basis at a Registered level by a comparatively small number of competitors; this perhaps points to a lack of facilities in some areas, for the level of interest among shooters is high and the major shoots are extraordinarily well patronised. During the 1988/89 season only a bare double handful of competitors shot over 2000 Registered targets at this discipline; the great majority shot well under 1000, comparatively few shooters returning averages exceeding 80 per cent. The shooter returning the highest number of Registered targets was J. Towell with 2240 for a class A/A average of 79.6 per cent – a remarkably consistent performance. Of those shooters returning 1000 or more targets, England team member George Digweed achieved the highest average of 91.2 per cent over his 1500 targets; he was one of a handful of shooters to exceed 90 per cent – an achievement in itself.

The future of English Sporting has never been brighter, and if facilities can match the level of interest among the shooting public, a boom sport will soon reach unprecedented heights.

9 FITASC Sporting

FITASC Sporting is the international Sporting discipline, governed by the Fédération Internationale de Tir aux Armes Sportives de Chasse. It differs from English Sporting in many ways, although the basic concept, especially in terms of the target types offered, remains very much the same. No better definition is to be found than that in the International Sporting Regulations – Article 1: 'Following the configuration of the grounds, a sporting layout must be equipped with a sufficient amount of traps so that the competitors will shoot under conditions as close as possible to game shooting – partridges, pheasants, ducks, rabbits, in front, low and high, crossing and quartering battue, in fields or in woods, hidden or not by trees and bushes.' Article 2 defines the targets to be used: 'The clays to be used are the regular trench, skeet and rabbit-shooting clays, thinner clays and clays with smaller diameter which have a higher speed, and possibly electric targets' (a long-winded way of saying, use anything!). In practice the organisers of FITASC Sporting shoots use a large number of non-standard targets. This provides greater variety and also tests the shooter to the utmost. In FITASC Sporting the shooter frequently encounters targets presented at the very limit of range, which is one reason why until recently $1\frac{1}{4}$ oz cartridge loads were commonly used. At most English Sporting grounds a 40-yards-plus target is an exception; in FITASC Sporting, if not exactly commonplace, it is most certainly encountered often enough not to raise eyebrows. This, then, sets the scene for FITASC Sporting, a varied and demanding discipline not to be attempted by the faint-hearted. It is a time-consuming, space-demanding and expensive form of the sport which tests the Sporting shooter to the limit.

THE RULES

For the most part the rules relating to FITASC Sporting, contained in CPSA Booklet No. 15 – International Sporting, correspond with those applying to English Sporting (see Chapter 8). However, the shooter should be aware of the following main variations.

Shooting Position

Article 3 The shooter will adopt the standing position, his feet within the limits of the shooting stand, his gun held with two hands clearly out of the shoulder. Gun touching the body under the armpit. He will keep this position until the bird or birds is in sight.

The departure of the birds is given by the Referee after the shooter has pronounced the word 'Ready'.

If the marksman positions himself wrongly or shoulders his gun before the target appears, he will receive a warning. A second fault will cause a 'No Bird' and if there is a third fault in the same run (sequence) a 'Nought' (Zero) will be called, or in the case of a double a 'Zero, Zero'.

Organisation of Competitions

Article 6 The shooting will occur in squads of a maximum of six shooters. If necessary it is permissible to form squads of at least three shooters.

Article 9 The shooting occurs in sequences of 25 or 30 birds . . .

Weapons and Ammunition

Article 22 The load of the cartridges may not exceed 36 grammes of shot. The cartridge must be normally loaded.

The result of the pair of shots when an irregular double is thrown (where one target is broken, etc.) differs from that outlined in the previous chapter, Rule 17, in the case of report pairs as follows:

Article 35 When shooting doubles 'on the gun', the following will be awarded:

(a)   Kill and 0 if the shooter breaks the first bird and misses the second.
(b)   Kill and No-bird, the double having to be shot again if:

   1   the shooter breaks the first bird and the second is irregular;
   2   the shooter breaks the first bird and a malfunction of his gun or misfire prevents him from shooting at his second bird;
   3   the shooter breaks the first bird but the second bird leaves late or not at all;
   4   the shooter breaks the first bird but the Referee prevents the shooter from firing his second shot owing to the violation of Article 3 providing the shooter has not already been warned for the same reason during the same 'round', otherwise the result of the first shot will be recorded and the second bird will be declared lost.

(c)   o and No-bird, the double having, however, to be shot again if the shooter misses the first bird and the second bird is irregular for one of the reasons given under (b).

THE LAYOUT

FITASC Sporting is a relatively slow discipline to shoot. As in other international disciplines, shooters operate in six-man squads and the targets are normally offered on individual twenty-five-target layouts presenting a wide variety of target types. Plenty of room is needed as the squad members are permitted to take their targets at any time between launch and subsequent landing, and it is therefore most certainly not a spectator sport; it also precludes shooters in following squads from viewing targets in advance. For this reason many of the large championships offer places for only some twelve to fourteen squads per day – sixty to seventy-two shooters – with perhaps three or four layouts working simultaneously. There are no defined specifications for FITASC Sporting beyond the fact that the shooting stand must be either a square measuring 0.91 m (2 feet 9 inches) on one side, or a circle measuring 1 metre (3 feet) in diameter. The shooter can fire at a target only while occupying the shooting stand. The only other stipulation is that defined in the latter part of Article 4: 'At each stand, the setting of the trajectories for all the shooters must be strictly the same in height, distance and speed.' The old principle in international shooting that each shooter should be offered the same targets is a good one, and ensures that an otherwise excellent shoot is not spoilt by accusations of unfairness.

Each layout consists of a number of traps, all set to offer differing targets; there is no repetition of targets, each one appearing differently as the squad moves from stand to stand. Individual layouts are often given specific names, and frequently consist of a high bias in favour of one type of target. For example, the Trench layout consists of a wide variety of low Trench-type targets; alternatively, the Tower layout may consist of a preponderance of high targets. The variety available is infinite, and as with English Sporting limited only by the imagination of the shoot organiser. In addition, on each layout there are several shooting stands, usually three or more, and the squad shoots them in order, rather in the manner of Skeet. However, in recognition of the fact that the person shooting first has less time to view the targets on offer and therefore less opportunity to work out angles and speeds, the squad shoots in rotation – something which occurs in no other discipline. Thus, using the example cited in Article 8: 'At each stand the six shooters of a squad will first fire at the single birds and, if necessary, the six shooters will then fire at the doubles. For example:

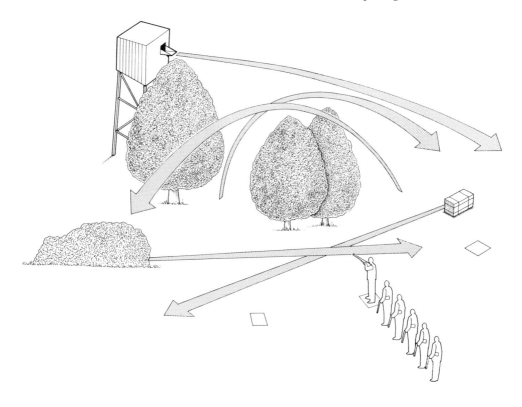

Stand 1 – a single – shooting in the following order: 1; 2; 3; 4; 5; 6.
Stand 1 – doubles – in the following order: 2; 3; 4; 5; 6; 1.
Stand 2 – singles – in the following order: 3; 4; 5; 6; 1; 2.
Stand 2 – doubles – in the following order: 4; 5; 6; 1; 2; 3.'

Figure 18 Sample FITASC Sporting layout with examples of target types and stands available

With single targets the shooter has full use of the gun (may fire both barrels at the target, with the result of either shot to count equally); with the doubles the shooter may fire both barrels at the first target if he so wishes (that is, if the first shot misses), although in this case the second target will be scored as a lost target.

EQUIPMENT

For equipment read the section on English Sporting. As explained above, the only major difference between the two disciplines is the extra ranges often encountered in the international version. Most shooters use the same sort of weapons as they would for English Sporting, the continuing trend towards longer-barrelled guns undoubtedly suiting the FITASC shooter. Ammunition may need to be of a more consistently higher grade when tackling FITASC, although there are few Sporting targets which cannot be dealt with adequately by a good-quality Trap cartridge; the use of nickel-coated loads may have some merit, although this is very much for the individual shooter to determine.

TECHNIQUE

Once again look at the comments contained in the last chapter. If there is any overriding advice for FITASC, it must surely be that the shooter must maintain concentration at all times. The single targets are every bit as important as the doubles, and need to be tackled with thought and determination if vital kills are not to slip away.

HIGH STANDARDS

Surprisingly perhaps, this discipline has the same qualifying percentage for the top class (A) as does the far easier domestic discipline – both having a cut-off point of 75 per cent. Further, there are only three classes, whereas all the other disciplines have four. It is still not widely available in Britain, with fewer than fifty shooters returning 1000 plus Registered targets. Of these, three shot the same high total of 1525 in 1989/90: D. Izzard (80 per cent), T. Westall (55.4 per cent) and K. Williamson (78.3 per cent). Of those shooters returning over 1000 targets, Mick Rouse had by far the highest average with 85.4 per cent (1150 targets); he was one of only six shooters to return over 80 per cent, which gives a good idea of the inherent problems involved in trying to achieve a good score at this discipline.

10 English Skeet

Skeet is a peculiarly un-English word, supposedly derived from the Scandinavian 'skyte' which roughly translated means 'to shoot'. Skeet appeared on the scene a good while after Trap, but soon attracted a cult following; it always has been, and will doubtless remain, a very keenly followed discipline. It provides a total contrast with the sheer unpredictability of Sporting. Of the Skeet variations, English Skeet is especially stereotyped, for every competitor knows that each and every target at every ground in the country must conform to rigid criteria; to a certain extent the same applies to Trap shooting, but in no other discipline is there the same degree of uniformity from bird to bird as that to be found in Skeet.

If Trap shooting is derived from live-pigeon shooting, and Sporting an attempt to duplicate wild quarry, Skeet is target shooting pure and simple, and on the face of it of little direct benefit to the quarry shooter – after all, on most days in the field it is very seldom that two identical targets are encountered, let alone a continual succession. Critics of Skeet say that it is boring and repetitive; repetitive it may be, boring never. Further, there can actually be a direct correlation between Skeet shooting and accurate shooting in the field.

In complete contrast to Sporting, a Skeet layout can seldom be constructed in any rough and ready *ad hoc* way. The layout must be precisely measured, and preferably solidly built. There are, of course, portable Skeet layouts made from wood and metal sheeting. But the tendency is for layouts to be solidly constructed from bricks and mortar. Because of this there will usually be a considerable degree of commitment on the part of those supplying the layouts, and it is most probable that strict competition rulings will apply. Even on practice days, the rules for English Skeet laid down by the CPSA will be in operation.

Indeed, the majority of English Skeet is shot under the auspices of CPSA-Registered competition. This is no bad thing, for it determines that standards are uniform throughout, which in turn helps shooters attain high levels of consistency. But because of the permanent nature of the layouts and the relatively slow throughput of Guns – three five-man squads an hour is about average – Skeet is not as widely available

as some other disciplines. Although it is immensely popular where it does occur, there is not, and indeed never can be, the same proliferation of layouts to be found in Sporting or, to a lesser extent, Down-the-Line.

THE RULES

The rules for Skeet are contained in CPSA Booklet No. 9. With regard to guns and ammunition, the same rules apply in all the domestic disciplines (see Chapter 8, Rule 3/4), with the exception of shot size as under Rule 19 '. . . or size larger than 2mm dia. (No.9 shot English)'. Similarly the rules applying to gun malfunctions (Chapter 8, Rule 16) are standard (although, curiously, worded differently).

Rule 21
One shot only may be fired at each target during its flight within the shooting bounds.

Rule 22
Shooting position: standing with both feet entirely within the boundary of the shooting. Gun position optional.

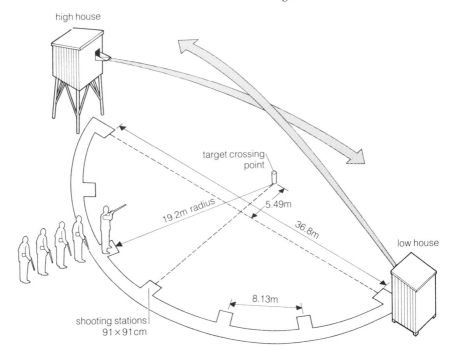

high house

target crossing point

19.2m radius

5.49m

36.8m

low house

8.13m

shooting stations
91 × 91 cm

Rule 23
When the shooter is ready he calls loudly ... some ... verbal command after which the target shall be thrown instantly.

Figure 19 English Skeet layout

It is worth noting here that the rules concerning standing entirely within the boundary of the shooting station and throwing the target instantly are common to all disciplines. Only in English Sporting, International Sporting and International Skeet is there a permissible delay in throwing the target.

Under most circumstances (with the exception of permissible malfunction and shooter error) the shooter must comply with:

Rule 30
(a)   ... the competitor MUST SHOOT A REGULAR DOUBLE to determine the result of both shots.

THE LAYOUT

As the illustration shows, the English Skeet layout is precisely engineered to present two different targets, one from a high house on the shooter's left, the other from a low house to the shooter's right. The targets are set to fly the same every time, that is, to travel over a central crossing point, which is offset 18 feet (5.49 m) from the base line between the two trap houses, and to land within a set distance –

164–170½ feet (50–52 m) – from the trap. The two target flight paths must converge at their central crossing point so that, height aside, they are in essence identical right-hand and left-hand targets. Before the start of every shoot the targets should always be 'hooped'. This hoop consists of a 3-foot (90 cm) diameter circle the *centre* of which is 15 feet (4.55 m) above the target crossing point – in essence a hoop on a pole designed to meet the above specifications.

From this it can be seen that there is a degree of flexibility in the presentation of a target; the variation can be as much as 6½ feet (2 m) in distance, and as much as 3 feet (0.9 m) in height. Such measurements may seem insignificant, but in real terms they may represent a noticeable variation in speed of target. In clear, still weather there should be no difficulty in setting targets to conform to these parameters, but when the weather turns inclement real problems may arise. Wind may play havoc with the targets. For example, a headwind will slow the targets, while causing them to climb inexorably upwards so that in extreme circumstances it is difficult to achieve both the required height and distance; similarly, a following wind will push targets down, again causing problems in making the distance. The greatest problem arises with a variable gusting wind, when targets vary wildly within a given round, which may prove most unfair on certain shooters. However, once the shoot organisers have set the targets as best they can, the shooters either have to accept the problem or go home.

Most experienced Skeet shooters understand this and are prepared to make allowances. But if there is no wind to muddle the equation there will certainly be recriminations if the targets are not just so. This is as it should be: all things being equal, the targets should conform to the parameters laid down.

As with any discipline, the same targets if shot from an identical position time and time again will soon become too easy and interest among shooters will rapidly wane. With Skeet the technique is simply to vary the shooter's position (as occurs with FITASC Sporting), which produces a wide range of angles and consequently an illusion of differing speed of target. This is achieved by shooting from different positions over a half-circle which arcs between high and low houses, with seven shooting stations used for English Skeet; at all times this half-circle maintains a constant radius of 63 feet from the target crossing point. Shooting stations start at number one directly below the exit point of the high-house target, and thereafter stations will be a fraction under 26 feet 8½ inches (8.13 m) apart at centre until one comes to station seven, positioned slightly to the left of the low-house target exit point. Target speed remains the same throughout, of course, but what does alter is the shooter's perception. This, then, is the craft of Skeet shooting: to 'read' each target for angle, and thereafter make the necessary adjustments to technique in order to achieve a kill.

EQUIPMENT

Having looked at the flight path of the target, and noted that speed and height remain a constant (windy conditions excepted), the shooter will then be faced with how to tackle the target itself. In Skeet, especially for the beginner, the perception of speed is infinitely greater than the reality. Skeet targets are close – on a consistent basis perhaps closer than those encountered in any other discipline. Trap targets do start off fairly close, but of course disappear rapidly away from the shooter – and the shooter must always bear this in mind. Therefore, he will need to address himself to the problem of hitting a close, relatively fast target.

With Skeet the trap and associated circuitry is wholly electrically operated, usually by a 12-volt system direct from a car battery, or alternatively via mains power and a volt transformer to bring the supply down to the required 12-volt level. With such a low power supply the trap is easily operated, which helps to produce consistent targets in terms of release and flight. Thereafter release of the target will be by the button-pusher, who invariably doubles as the referee. If he is an experienced person good, quick, consistent releases are guaranteed. Indeed, this is vital if consistently high scores are to be achieved – in English Skeet when the shooter calls for the target it should come instantly (Rule 23 clearly states that '. . . the target shall be thrown instantly'). The days of manually released traps are fortunately long gone; in their place are either manually cocked and loaded versions with the electric release or, increasingly, fully automatic magazine-fed traps. To the shooter there may be no great difference, although in general terms a fully automated system – once it has been run in and any wrinkles ironed out – should provide better and more trouble-free service in the long run. As in most things, once the human element has been removed there is usually less room for error.

The target presentation is worth a brief mention here, for it really does relate closely to any subsequent consideration of gun and ammunition and, of course, shooting techniques. Although this presentation is uniform, and therefore predictable, and the target is mostly 20 yards or less – for practical shooting purposes never more than 40 yards – it is always a small end-on target with dimensions of approximately 180 mm by 26 mm. This in reality means a thin black sliver knifing through the air with a speed which can be quite alarming for the beginner – a small, fast-moving target which allows little room for error. The illusory speed is relevant to the shooter's position on the layout: on the centre stands (3–5) the target reveals its true speed,

Shooting at Clays

while on the end stands (1, 2, 6, 7) the target may seem either ultra-fast (out-going target) or ultra-slow (in-coming target). The shooter taken in by these illusions is heading for a missed target.

Throughout the history of Skeet shooting, manufacturers of guns and equipment have worked relentlessly to produce a range of paraphernalia which will satisfy the discerning shooter in his quest for a perfect Skeet-shooting combination. Whether such perfection actually exists is open to doubt. Unquestionably there are given criteria which fulfil most requirements, but these are still subject to the whim of the individual shooter. The actual variety of killing combinations is considerable, although admittedly within certain parameters. Even more confusingly, Skeet shooters' requirements seem to be in a state of on-going evolution, with fashion trends sometimes having as much bearing on what is being used as actual killing capability. Admittedly some of these trends are initiated by the shooting fraternity itself in response to a particular need, but equally often the manufacturers influence shooters with the 'hard sell' – after all, it is firmly in their interests to encourage this evolutionary process. This works to the advantage of the shooter in that many of the products on offer are subject to constant improvement in a highly competitive market, something which is especially true of guns.

However, in terms of pellet size at least, ammunition is one facet of Skeet shooting which has remained fairly constant over the years. Rule 19 states that the pellet size should not be larger than number 9 shot English (2 mm in diameter): this is historically the commonly used size, although some shooters do use 9½s or even 10s. Number 9 shot undoubtedly patterns well from most guns, throwing a wide yet evenly spread pattern over the close ranges encountered in this discipline; at these ranges even an individual pellet retains sufficient energy to break a clay target, and although it is most satisfying to see a target disappear into a plume of black dust, even a single minute chip will count as a kill. 'They all count' is a phrase commonly heard after a particularly chippy kill, and this can often be a source of amusement; even though it will count the same as a dusted target, it betrays a fault in either technique or timing – sometimes both – and a missed target often follows soon afterwards. Alternatively, the experienced shooter may see this as a warning, and thereafter will sharpen up and get back into a smooth killing mode.

Whatever the problems encountered on the Skeet range, these can seldom be attributable to the cartridges, all the popularly used and commonly available brands being very similar in most respects. Some brands are faster than others, although often differences are minimal. However, there is an undeniable advantage for the shooter using a crisp quick load in that this may affect the manner in which the target is addressed. This is a facet of Skeet shooting which can be learnt only from experience. Cartridge choice is very much a case of individual preference, and it is not possible to say which is 'best'; the 'best' cartridge for one shooter may be absolute rubbish to another.

Guns fall into a similar category, and the variety to be seen on any large Skeet shoot will probably be as wide as that available on the market. Many of those who shoot this discipline to the exclusion of all else do use specialist Skeet guns, which will invariably be an open-choked, short-barrelled, sweet-handling over-and-under; these will have been designed to provide the very best in the fast handling which many shooters see as vital when dealing with these close targets. Not many years ago almost all specialised Skeet guns possessed 25-inch or 26-inch barrels, the trend of the day dictating that this was the type of weapon best suited to the discipline. This was unquestionably linked to the evolutionary process alluded to above. Whether this specification was the best is open to doubt; the fact that shooters are now moving away from the short-barrelled specialist type reinforces the argument of those who maintained that short barrels were if anything counter-productive. It is an argument for which there can never be any definitive answer; once again it is strictly horses for courses. Some shooters perform miraculously with this type of weapon; an equal number perform well with more traditional guns.

The open choke is widely accepted by many shooters as desirable, if not absolutely essential, for the discipline. Indeed, the 'Skeet' specification in chokes is widely understood in shooting circles. In essence it is a refinement on the true cylinder theme, which is in fact no choke at all; improved cylinder (approximately $\frac{1}{4}$ choke) is also widely used, while some outstanding Shots use even tighter chokings. The experienced shooter can use tighter chokes without any noticeable fall-off in scores, but for the beginner or less gifted Shot the use of very open chokes is to be strongly recommended. Tinkering with chokes is an on-going process; a fairly recent attempt to produce an elliptical choke, which will throw a pattern designed to pick out that speeding narrow sliver of clay, is still to be widely adopted; whether it is simply another stage in the process of evolution remains to be seen.

The general trend towards longer-barrelled guns, referred to in the chapters dealing with the Sporting disciplines, is also to be found in the Skeet world, with 28-inch barrels now common and even 30-inch barrels not unheard of. The trend of dropping the short-barrelled fast-handling weapon in favour of a heavier, more pointable long-barrelled gun continues and has much in its favour – doubly so in the case of the casual Skeet shooter who perhaps uses a single gun for a multiplicity of purposes. As with Sporting, a general-purpose field weapon can give sterling service, and no shooter should feel inhibited for lack of a specialist Skeet gun. The widely used general-purpose Sporter/Sporting/Field gun can be used with great success. If it has the multi-choke facility so much the better. Semi-automatic shotguns were at one time very popular among Skeet shooters, some very notable champions winning their titles with just such weapons; the lightness and all-round well-balanced features of most semi-automatics make them ideally suited for Skeet, the above comments about choke holding good for these guns, too. Some manufacturers produced purpose-designed Skeet semi-autos, with the Americans probably leading the field; indeed, the Remington 1100 was one of the most successful and widely used of all Skeet semi-autos. These guns are still to be seen in action today, but in view of the problems surrounding semi-auto ownership, basically engendered by the Firearms (Amendment) Act, 1988, and a growing aversion to such weapons, we sadly can probably expect to see less and less of them. The same thing applies to the pump-action weapon, though this was never much favoured by Skeet practitioners in Britain anyway. In the United States it is a widely used and accepted weapon right across the spectrum of shotgun shooting sports.

The traditional clay shooter's waistcoat is generally known as a Skeet vest, and in its most basic form consists of a sleeveless waistcoat with shoulder pad and large pockets. Skeet, by its very nature, calls for the shooter to be a neatly packaged unit, ideally carrying everything he may need with him. This has led to the development of a vest which allows the shooter to carry the twenty-five cartridges needed for a full round, a few spares for broken targets, etc., plus a whole host of other odds and ends. Various designs are available, a Skeet vest of some description being widely recognised as an essential part of the uniform. Shooting glasses, designed to highlight the sliver of a target against what may be a bright background sky, are favoured by some shooters, as is a large-peaked cap which can also help to reduce glare. Ear defenders, gloves, etc. are also variously favoured, and as with gun types there may be a seemingly infinite variety on any one shoot.

TECHNIQUE

The illusory effect of the targets throughout the layout has already been referred to. In practice the seven stands will be shot in the following sequence.

Station 1: two singles and a double
Station 2: two singles and a double
Station 3: two singles
Station 4: two singles and a double (with the first target to be nominated by the shooter)
Station 5: two singles
Station 6: two singles and a double
Station 7: two singles and a double

This gives us twenty-four targets in all. The twenty-fifth needed to complete a full round will be either a repeat of the first missed target, or else in the event of no misses throughout the twenty-four it will be either the high-house target or the low-house target from station 7 – the option being the shooter's. With all single targets the high-house target must be shot first on every occasion. With doubles the high-house target must be shot on stations 1 and 2; station 4 is optional, as referred to above, while the low-house target must be taken first from stations 6 and 7.

In English Skeet gun position before firing is optional; that is, the shooter can opt either for the more relaxed gun-down position, or for the gun-mounted position favoured by Trap shooters. The gun-down position is the most widely preferred, but the gun-mounted position does find favour with some and may be particularly useful for the beginner as it lessens the likelihood of any error in gun mounting – a common reason for missing on the part of newcomers to the sport. Another noteworthy point is that it is permissible to load only one cartridge at a time for the singles on each stand; this can also be a useful tool for the shooter in that it seems to encourage deliberate, thoughtful shooting, allowing as it does a valuable few seconds for collecting the thoughts between each single shot.

With all Skeet, and here English Skeet is no exception, most experienced shooters break the target on or before the central crossing point. The reasons for this are fairly straightforward: by this central crossing point the target is still near maximum velocity and is in level flight – to delay long after that central crossing point means that the shooter is forced to deal with a slowing, dropping target; in windy conditions the problems associated with delaying in firing may be multiplied many fold as the target behaves demonically. Therefore, if there is a golden rule for Skeet shooting, it must surely be to take the target as soon as is reasonably practical. The instinctive type of shooter, particularly the one who uses the maintained-lead method, falls into this trap less frequently; it is the shooter who uses the tracking and overtaking method who is theoretically more likely to be lured into delaying too long. As with all forms of shooting, there is an optimum time for taking the target, and with Skeet it is most definitely on or near the centre. However, particularly for the beginner, this is much easier said than done, and constant practice will be needed in order to perfect this technique.

If we accept that ideally the target should be shot at this stage, we can next address a further two fundamental governing factors: how to stand and where to point the gun. The importance of these two factors cannot be overstated. Both are equally crucial if broken targets are to be the norm. As with Sporting, the shooter should always stand with the leading foot pointed towards the place where he expects to break

Andy Harvison displays the classic gun hold position/stance in the shoot-off for High Gun at the 1990 British Open Skeet Championship

the target. The shooter's weight will be thrown forward slightly on to this foot, which becomes the pivotal point for the body. All actions thereafter will hinge on the correctness or otherwise of this stance. The majority of shooters favour a narrow stance, that is, standing fairly upright with the feet only a foot or so apart. Of course, there are exceptions to this, some shooters adopting the most outlandish of styles. Because these may work well for them, there is no real basis for criticism. But such excesses are not to be recommended for the beginner. Having taken up this narrow stance it is now natural to point the gun in the same direction as that leading foot, so that the whole body, from the feet up through to the hands holding the gun, takes up a comfortable position addressing the area where the shot will be directed. At the same time, the shooter must keep the line of the muzzles below the expected line of flight of the target in order to avoid missing above. Now, by twisting the body to point the gun towards the area where the target will first be observed – i.e. a few feet out from the target exit point on the relevant trap house (*not at the exit point itself*, as this is too far back and will result in the shooter frantically chasing the target) – it will be easy and natural to pick up the target and rotate the body back to its former comfortable position, at the same time pointing, swinging and firing the gun at the appropriate time. Easy! However, unless the stance and gun position are right in the first instance, everything else will be awry; and the shooter is likely to be disorientated and is always going to struggle to catch and break the target.

As with any other discipline, there is no discernible advantage obtainable from using maintained-lead or follow-through styles other than that the maintained-lead style may be a little quicker. It is strictly a matter for the individual, and the most successful shooter will always be the one who has best adapted his own style to suit the prevailing circumstances. The differing styles may affect the amount of *perceivable* lead given to the target in order to achieve a hit, but again it is a matter of individual interpretation. I stress the word 'perceivable' advisedly, simply because each shooter sees the target differently and thus their perception of the technique needed to smash that target may vary considerably from that of other shooters. Some shooters – myself included – have a clear notion of how much lead is needed for success against each target; others may believe that they are shooting directly at the target when in fact the speed of swing takes up the necessary lead. They are two differing techniques, both with a common end – the successful breaking of the target.

Station 1

The high-house single. With this high-house target the shooter stands directly below the exit point of the target; although it is in level flight, as are all such targets, it gives the impression of rapidly dropping. Despite this it is a straightforward target, yet it is surprisingly missed from time to time by some very experienced shooters. The technique is to take up the line of the target with the muzzles, and thereafter draw up the barrels until they are pointed at something like a 45-degree angle; after the launch of the target the barrels need only drop on the line of the target a fraction until it can be clearly seen above the muzzle – this is the moment to fire. In other words, the shooter must fire below the target; any delay at this point will almost certainly result in a miss. As with all Skeet targets, a smooth precise action is essential. Any delay or hanging on the target is likely to result in a miss.

The low-house single. The muzzles should be pointed slightly to the left of target exit point, a low point position being maintained. The target, which will first be seen a few feet out from the low house, is arguably one of the easiest of the twenty-four; yet, as with all easy targets, it is quite missable if the shooter fails to maintain maximum concentration. For most of its flight this target seems very slow moving, almost floating over the central crossing point; unless taken very late it is a target which requires minimal lead, and should simply be blotted out and broken around the centre by keeping the gun moving. If there is a perceivable lead it is no more than a few inches.

The double. This is simply a combination of the two single targets; indeed, this has to be the way of taking all doubles – as two single targets. Above all else the shooter needs to acquire a patient, unflustered style which will ruthlessly despatch both targets in succession. The understandable tendency among newcomers for rushing the first target in order to allow plenty of time for the second can frequently result in a first-barrel miss, followed by a complete disruption in timing and the missing of the second target, too – in short, total disaster entirely due to rushing that first target. For success the shooter must address the high-house target in the normal manner, calling for and breaking the target; assuming it has been broken somewhere in the region of the central crossing point, it merely remains to turn left-handed for the low-house target as it floats up to the shooter's left hand. Few shooters let the gun out of the shoulder for the second shot on the doubles, preferring instead to move smoothly on to the target with the natural body movement; there is no need to hurry the shot even though the target is very close indeed, the lead being in the order of 12 inches. At all costs avoid being lulled into stopping the swing by the apparent slowness of the target.

Station 2
The high-house single. For me this is one of the two hardest targets on any Skeet layout (the other being low-house 6). As with station 1, there is still a slight perception of a dropping target, but now a tricky quartering angle is introduced; the upshot of this combination is a target which seems to fly with an awesome speed sufficient to cause near-panic in the newcomer. Again calmness is the order of the day: settle quietly on the shooting position with both front foot and muzzles pointing slightly to the left of centre, and turn body and muzzles back towards the high-house until the muzzles point a few feet out from the exit point. When the target appears between exit point and muzzles, stay calm, swing with the target and fire the instant the required 12–18-inch lead has been taken up – do not delay firing for even a moment. In effect you will be shooting down the right-hand side of the target, and if all movements are coordinated correctly the target will break on or near the centre. It is especially important with this target to

keep the muzzles below the line of flight before calling, as this will discourage a strong tendency to shoot over.

The low-house single. Like the previous low-house target, this is an easy enough challenge. Many shooters prefer to alter their foot position for each high- or low-house target, with a corresponding adjustment to muzzle point. This is frequently carried out during reloading and is an ideal way of concentrating on the job in hand. Even if a shooter does not alter his foot position he may shuffle about as an almost subconscious mechanism for steadying himself for the next target. So long as the correct foot/muzzle position is maintained there should be no problem in spotting the target just after it leaves the exit point, and thereafter in swinging on to the target and firing the instant the necessary 2-foot lead has been attained. The target is going to seem fairly slow moving, although less so than on station 1, and so long as the shooter gives this his full concentration and does not take the shot for granted it should present few problems.

The double. Once again these must be treated as two singles. Ignore the fact that on call both targets are launched simultaneously, and concentrate on that difficult high-house target. So long as this is shot as outlined above, there will be no impediment to coming back instantly, yet smoothly, for the low-house target, which by now will have passed the centre. There is still plenty of time to complete the pair, and this will be accomplished with ease so long as the swing is smooth and there is no tendency either to hurry or to stop the gun.

Station 3

The high house. This is in many ways a much easier target than its immediate predecessor, mainly because it has lost the quartering element and appears as a crossing target which more closely reflects the true speed of these Skeet targets. It is fairly quick, yet more easily read. Once again the front foot/muzzle position should be addressing the place where the target will be broken, with that left-hand rotation bringing the muzzle back towards the exit point. For me this target requires a lead of around 3 feet as a reflection of the greater perceived speed. Nothing to worry about so long as earlier lessons have not been forgotten.

The low house. This target is as quick as any to be found in a round of Skeet, although, lacking the angles encountered on station 2 (high house) and 6 (low house), it can lull the shooter into a false sense of security. Again faultless positioning is essential, while a lead of approaching 4 feet will reflect the speed encountered. With no double to worry about, it is important to concentrate on what is on offer.

Station 4

The high house. Another quick target requiring a 4-foot lead. Follow the previous advice to the letter, for shooting a round of Skeet 25-straight is all about total concentration on every single target. There are no illusions here to confuse the shooter, just an obviously quick target. Any foul-up will be due to faulty technique, usually manifested in a slow swing or a checking of the swing.

The low house. Same again: 4-foot lead, a smooth, continuous swing through the target, and another satisfying ball of black dust. Once again beware of the target's ability to outpace you.

The double. This is undoubtedly the most difficult of the doubles on offer, success being absolutely dependent on good technique. The option of high-house or low-house target first can concern the newcomer, who is likely to chop and change constantly. In reality, so long as conditions are relatively still, the right-handed shooter is well advised always to take the high-house target first as the body will swing naturally back from right to left for the second shot. Target address should be as above, with the swing and resultant shot smoothly and precisely executed. The low-house target will already be airborne of course, and this too is every bit as quick as its high-house counterpart; although the shooter must bear this in mind, it should in no way detract from the determination to break that high target first. After seeing the high-house target break, the shooter must bring the gun back instantly for the low-house target, which by now will be well on its way towards the high house. It is important to establish a routine for breaking this second target as soon as possible, as the perception alters the further it flies. The shooter fires along the left-hand side of the target, taking up a lead of perhaps a couple of feet depending on how far it has flown – in some cases, according to conditions, it may be necessary to shoot slightly under the target as it begins to drop.

When it is windy the shooter may need to alter his treatment of this double. If the wind is strong he would be wise to take first whichever target is being wind assisted, otherwise the second shot may become something of a lottery, the target either dipping or climbing sharply. This may also wildly affect the manner in which the shooter addresses questions of foot position and target lead. With so many imponderables it is not possible to offer worthwhile advice. Only experience will teach the shooter how to come to terms with different conditions, and this really can be a lifetime's work; nevertheless, given a basically sound technique the shooter will usually be able to overcome such variables. Indeed, for anyone with championship aspirations this sort of adaptability is essential.

Station 5

The high house. A tricky target this, for it is here that the targets begin to lose the character of the true crosser and start to recreate the sort of confusing illusions encountered on earlier stands. This target seems to be moving deceptively slowly and will be missed behind, time without number, by the beginner; it appears to creep down the range, and unless the shooter displays great determination the opportunity to break the target at the centre will be lost. Point both front foot and muzzles at the central crossing point, move the muzzles slightly back towards the high house and call; do not be deceived, but move the muzzles through the target and fire when a lead of around 3 feet has been attained. Above all, keep the gun moving.

The low house. This target is also deceptive, at least as deceptive as the high-house target. It rushes down the range offering the most obtuse of oblique angles and the shooter needs to stand correctly and shoot well inside the line of flight if the requisite 3-foot lead is to be taken up. Again beware of hanging on the target or of pointing *at* the target; either will almost certainly result in a miss behind.

Station 6

The high house. For me this is one of the easier targets, but it is also one which can deceive with its apparently slow flight. A great many shooters who should know better let this target right in close before firing; as with any target in any discipline, the cardinal sin of hanging on the target is a prime cause of missing, and this one is no exception. A lead of a couple of feet will break the target shortly after it passes the centre, although if it is taken later it will be very close and seemingly moving much faster.

The low house. For me a potentially very difficult target, although probably this is attributable to a weakness in my own technique. Many times my straight has ended with low-house 6! Foot/muzzle position should be towards the centre, with the target speeding away from a point not much more than 25 feet from your right elbow. At all costs avoid the tendency to snatch at the target, or to shoot it straight up the rear. The target must be led, albeit by no more than 12 inches; be sure to fire inside the line – but not too far inside, as this is an easy one to miss in front.

The double. On the low-house side of the range the low-house target must be shot first on the doubles. Therefore, adopt the same positions and attitude as outlined for the single target. As ever, take care of this one first, and so long as the low-house target is taken crisply the high-house target will be there for the taking. Simply swing back on the line of the target, take on the 2-foot lead necessary for a break, pull the trigger and keep the gun moving. Easy!

Station 7

Having got this far the shooter really should shoot straight. Any lapse at this point will almost always be brought about by a lack of concentration. All four targets are easy enough so long as they are not treated with contempt. Plenty of targets have been missed on station 7, but always remember that many more have been broken and there is no reason to suppose that you will fail.

The high house. An easy target coming almost directly at you, but even so, watch it! Position should be held just to the right of centre. All that is needed is to settle quietly on the station, take up position and call; blot out the in-coming target and with the very minimum of lead see it break. Avoid hanging on the target.

The low house. Another easy target, ejecting 3 feet away from the right elbow with a clang of the trap, and missed only through sloppiness and incorrect target address. The aim should be to shoot the target in the rear, but beware of missing either over the top or inside the line of flight – both common faults. The muzzles must be held slightly below the line of flight; thereafter call for the target, raise and fire all in one movement. Again, avoid pointing in order to make sure.

The double. An easy double if ever there was one, with the shooter simply taking up the position needed for the low-house single. Under no circumstances rush that first shot; see it break and swing back for the high target, which by now will be rushing in with surprising speed, although because it is so close it will need no more than a couple of feet lead. Having shot all twenty-four targets, the twenty-fifth must now be taken at the shooter's discretion. Choice of target is optional and both are easy enough – after all, they have just been broken twice over. The only real prospect of a miss at this stage will be from an attack of nerves, something which is all too common with relative newcomers. The experienced Skeet shooter should never miss at this stage, and seldom does.

NSSA SKEET

This Skeet variant is the least commonly encountered form in Britain today, being almost exclusively confined to those military establishments on which American personnel are based. The North American Skeet Association practises Skeet on a large scale and it is pursued with vigour by many ex-patriates based in this country. In form it is

almost identical to English Skeet, with the notable exception that there is no double on station 4 and the extra targets are instead taken up by the addition of a station 8. For comments on station 8 refer to the next chapter dealing with ISU Skeet, where station 8 is also a feature. The technique required for this variant is therefore very much the same as that described above. The other notable innovation adopted by the Americans is the widespread use of smaller-calibre shotguns: 20-bore, 28-bore and .410 are all widely used, and despite the high degree of marksmanship required when using such small weapons with their tiny patterns, the scores returned are still amazingly high. It is a variant well worth seeking out, and is every bit as enjoyable as English Skeet.

Nearly there! Jim Munday on the verge of the 1990 British Skeet title

HIGH STANDARDS

Today some incredible shooting feats are recorded in English Skeet, virtually every major championship being won with 100-straight. Many attribute this to the uniformity of the targets and the fact that with practice and application the top Shots can break every target with a fair degree of regularity. This may well be so, although the fact that

97

there is not a glut of 100-straights in competition – even though most competitors are capable of the feat – suggests that the inherent pressure of big competition is a significant regulating factor. Calls to make English Skeet more difficult do not, in my opinion, hold much water. Nevertheless it would be fair to state that the major events are essentially staged in two phases: the competition, during which everyone shoots to attain their best possible score, and the subsequent shoot-off among those achieving 100-straight.

An insight into the sort of dedication necessary to attain and retain high standards in English Skeet may be gained by a glance through the CPSA Members' Averages book for the period 1989/90. The two men to shoot most registered English Skeet targets were C.A. Bennett, who shot 4700 targets for an average of 91.2 per cent (A class), and D. Shaw, also with 4700 targets for an average of 93.8 per cent (A/A class). Curiously perhaps, it is noteworthy that in the same period Martin Elworthy – British Champion for 1987, 1988 and 1989 and English Champion for 1990 – shot only 725 targets, yet his average was an incredible 99.5 per cent: obviously the work of a very gifted Skeet shooter.

11 ISU Skeet

THE RULES

Many of the rules relating to English Skeet transpose themselves to the ISU discipline (see CPSA Booklet No. 12 – International Skeet). In English Skeet only one cartridge may be loaded for single targets, whilst in ISU the rule dealing with number of cartridges is specific.

Rule 6.7

(a)   On Station 1 only one cartridge may be loaded to shoot the high house single target.

(b)   On Stations 2, 3, 4, 5, and 6 two cartridges must be loaded to shoot the single targets . . .

(c)   On Station 8 only one cartridge may be loaded to shoot at the target emerging from the high house. After firing on that target another cartridge may be loaded for the low house target.

(d)   During single target shooting with the gun loaded with two cartridges, the shooter must not open his gun after shooting the first of the two singles . . .

(e)   Only on Stations 1 and 8 may the shooter raise his gun to his shoulder and sight for a few seconds, both for single and double targets and on Station 8 both for the high house and low house targets . . .

THE LAYOUT

The layout used for ISU Skeet is identical to that used for English Skeet and is to be found fully specified in Chapter 8. The only variations concern the actual presentation of the target, and even though the same broad parameters as English Skeet apply, the changes are significant enough to make a great deal of difference to the way in which the shooter treats the sport. There are four main variations on the English Skeet theme: target speed is greatly increased; an additional stand is included, making eight in all; there is a variable delay on target release; and the shooter *must* adopt a gun-down position until the target has been released. These four variations are what makes ISU Skeet such a substantially greater challenge than

English Skeet and, as will be seen, they demand greater consistency from the shooter in terms of technique.

The target speed will prove to be the greatest initial problem for the shooter reared on a diet of English Skeet. As already mentioned, the actual physical dimensions and construction of the layout are the same; the central crossing point and the height of the hoop through which the target must pass also remain the same, but the target itself passes through the hoop much faster and needs to carry 213 feet 3 inches (65 m), and crucially must be broken within the confines of the layout rather than after it has passed either high house or low house. To ensure that this latter ruling is complied with, line judges are appointed for each squad and this really can make a difference, especially on the doubles; to all intents and purposes line judges must be considered an integral part of the layout, and may make all the difference to the shooter if his reactions are that little bit slower on any particular target. Variations in height at the central crossing point are still allowed, but distance stipulations are fairly precise in order to maintain that extra speed.

The extra stand – station 8 – is positioned exactly in the centre of the layout between the high house and the low house, that is, on the base chord with the centre of the stand 60 feet 4½ inches (18.4 m) from each trap house. The stand itself must be 6 feet by 3 feet (1.83 m by 0.91 m), that is, twice the length of the other shooting stands. The provision of an electrical timer in the release mechanism allows for the random release of targets on demand at intervals of anything from

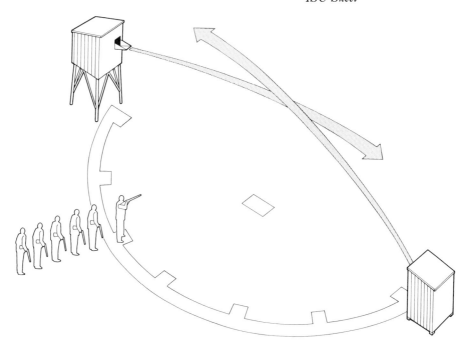

Figure 20
International Skeet
layout

instantaneous to three seconds. Thus the same electrical circuitry as used in English Skeet can be used for ISU, with the timer usually being engaged at the flick of a switch.

EQUIPMENT

There is no great need for a change in anything other than technique for ISU Skeet, and most of the comments relevant to English Skeet apply. However, it is not uncommon for more expensive top-grade ammunition to be used, any extra speed of shot being gratefully accepted as the shooter struggles to come to terms with those super-fast targets. The competitor must complete each round with the same type of cartridge with which it was begun. The guns seldom differ greatly, although the casual observer may be surprised to find that there is not a greater tendency to go for lighter guns as a response to the faster targets; even then, any variation is more likely to come about as the result of individual preference rather than any genre trend.

TECHNIQUE

The inclusion of an extra shooting station means that there is a different sequence for taking targets, and this appears as follows:

Station 1: one single from the high house and a double
Station 2: two singles and a double

Station 3: two singles and a double
Station 4: two singles
Station 5: two singles and a double
Station 6: two singles and a double
Station 7: one double
Station 8: two singles

Thus, there are a full twenty-five targets, with no optional target necessary to make up the number. Also, there is scarcely an easy target to be had: no bankers or almost guaranteed targets as can be found in English Skeet, but a round which needs to be worked for by concentration and solid application. The shooter will be well advised to follow the advice offered in the previous chapter, although a sharper addressing of targets and slightly increased leads would be advisable to deal with the extra speed encountered. The removal of such targets as the low target on station 1 and the singles on station 7 does much to raise the tempo, while the inclusion of doubles on stations 3 and 5 and the addition of station 8 ensure that the shooter remains alert at all times. The removal of the double on station 4 allows room for the introduction of the two singles on station 8; the inclusion of the doubles on stations 3 and 5 are likely to challenge the shooter far more as the angles found on these two stations are likely to cause many more problems. If there is any single overriding piece of advice worth offering, it is that the shooter concentrate on his follow-through more than ever before; this can be seen in an exaggerated form in some shooters, but it most certainly prevents the dreaded syndrome of stopping the gun from creeping in.

Station 8

Dealing with station 8 is something of a nightmare for the beginner, for with that gun-down position the target seems to come almost before the shooter has time to move. However, it is all a question of practice. Watch a good shooter tackle the target and it becomes obvious that there is, in fact, plenty of time. The muzzles should be held well out from the target exit point, so that as soon as the target is seen the gun can move smoothly up for the killing shot; there is no time for deliberation and the gun must be fired the instant it comes into the shoulder if the target is not to beat the shooter for speed; it means that this shot perhaps more than any other is instinctively fired at a racing target. It is doubtful if any lead can be visualised on this target, but it is vitally important to keep the gun moving in order to ensure that the target is not missed behind; it is also vital to ensure that the gun keeps moving as the trigger is pulled. It is all too easy to poke at this target, with the resultant miss behind. The same applies to both high-house and low-house targets; if anything, the low-house target may be

slightly more difficult as the lower trajectory will mean that it is picked up that split-second later.

The mandatory gun-down position is the fourth major factor which distinguishes ISU Skeet as a discipline. The ruling on this matter is quite clear and is covered succinctly in the relevant CPSA booklet No. 12, *Rules and Regulations for International Skeet*, under 6.5a: 'Until the target appears the competitor must stay in the ready position, holding the gun with both hands so that the gun butt touches the crest of the hip bone.' Article 6.5b elaborates by stating that the referee can be aided in controlling this facet of ISU shooting by the provision of a mark – approximately 4 inches long by 3/4 inch wide (10 cm by 2 cm) – in the appropriate position on the outside of the shooter's garment – usually the Skeet vest. The gun-ready position is clearly demonstrated by both the accompanying line drawing and the photograph.

Other ISU rulings may also affect the shooter's attitude towards this discipline, and may well have an effect on technique and scores, particularly if the shooter is more used to English Skeet. The ready position is reinforced by the ruling which disallows sightings of targets, or the mounting of the gun by way of practice on any but stations 1 and 8. Similarly, the ruling calling for the loading of two cartridges where two single targets exist – on stations 2, 3, 4, 5 and 6 – with no breaking of the gun allowed, can be disconcerting at first. The methodical, thoughtful loading of a single cartridge in between single targets can prove a great aid to the concentration of the English Skeet shooter – but of course, the ISU shooter will have his own aids to concentration.

Concentrating on
the next target

The very nature of Skeet in all its forms calls for a mentality closely allied to that of the Sporting shooter, with significant breaks in shooting allowing for broken concentration if the shooter is not on his guard. The absence of the intense concentration needed on the Trap line means that Skeet shooters seem to adapt to a technique of intense concentration for shorter spells immediately before walking on to the shooting station. The very fact that the shooters have to move about between stations means that concentration techniques must be flexible, and these in turn vary markedly from one individual to the next: some shooters remain quietly aloof from their fellows during station changes; some seem relaxed and even chatty; some pace about in an agitated manner; others may go off to one side and patiently and quietly await their turn to shoot. Increased pressure as the competition hots up may also have its effect, and this may be detectable by the shooters' reactions in between stations. ISU Skeet shooters are as subject to pressure as any other shooters, perhaps more so when one

considers that a Great Britain place may ultimately be at stake.

The constituent members of the actual six-man shooting squad may also have a bearing on the performance of individuals. With all domestic disciplines shooters may shoot with whom they like, and shooting with people they know may have an effect on scores; with ISU there is a draw to determine who shoots with whom. In this way any psychological advantage gained by shooting with 'friends' is negated. After the first day's competition the squads are re-formed so that like is squadded with like: the shooters with the lower scores are put together and shoot first on the day; by natural progression the shooters with the best scores shoot last, an arrangement which guarantees excitement and drama right up to the end of the competition. This in its turn may influence the mental approach of the shooter, although the top shooters may well gain a psychological boost from shooting together so often in the final squads.

Figure 21 Gun ready position for ISU Skeet and FITASC Sporting

HIGH STANDARDS

ISU Skeet is unquestionably one of the ultimate tests in clay shooting, something which is reflected in the generally low scores. Yet, as ever, the top shooters do turn in some remarkable scores, despite the comparative dearth of facilities. The latter shortage is evident in the scores shown in the CPSA Members' Averages book, no shooter recording 3000 Registered targets. In competitive terms, under 3000

Registered targets in a year is fairly low, and this lack of facilities does Britain's international prospects no good at all. The difficulty of ISU can also be seen in the percentages dividing the different classes: for the top class (A) the dividing line is 88 per cent. The comparison with English Skeet with a class A/A dividing line of 94 per cent speaks volumes.

After the 1990 English Grand Prix for ISU Skeet the leading shooters were headed by Ken Harman, with the Grand Prix winner Andy Austin lying third. Harman and Austin have been among the top ISU shooters for several seasons now, and although both can undoubtedly produce the goods on the big occasion the Averages book tells an interesting tale: Harman has barely made class A with 88.2 per cent over 1400 targets, whereas Austin is one of the few ISU shooters to record an average above 90 per cent, his average of 94.6 per cent over 1050 targets being over 1 per cent better than his nearest rival. Although the contention that practice makes perfect is often irrefutable, it is perhaps significant that those with the most targets to their credit are ranged throughout the lower classes – the shooter with the highest number of recorded targets is in fact in class C with slightly less than 80 per cent – surely further evidence that ISU really is a very difficult sport.

12 Down-the-Line

For many shooters Down-the-Line in its simplest form means any target which rises in front and thereafter flies more or less directly away. In essence this definition is true enough, although advocates of this discipline would consider it somewhat derogatory and in practice it is a long way from the truth. Undeniably DTL is often the sort of target favoured by beginners. There are inevitably fewer demands on technique, and such recurring nightmares for the novice as gun mount will be less critical in the first encounters. It is true to say that target for target this sort of clay presentation produces arguably the easiest of all clays, and for this reason alone they are ideal for the beginner.

The first appearance of DTL was around 1892, and right from the outset it proved popular; its popularity continues to this day, when only English Sporting is more universally followed. A glance at the CPSA Members' Averages book confirms that DTL has a huge following, while many other shooters also participate without having their names recorded. Such popularity may well stem from the superficial ease with which even the newcomer can soon graduate to producing some fairly good scores; yet the difference between achieving good scores, with the occasionally excellent total thrown in, and consistently returning the sort of top-class scores needed to gain championship or inter-national honours is immense. The individual target may not be especially difficult, but the task of stringing a hundred good kills together under the intense pressure of competition shooting is another story altogether. It is the never-ending search for true and lasting consistency which provides the real answer to why so many shooters persist for so long in shooting such 'easy' targets.

Today's DTL shooter finds a strictly regimented discipline where the targets conform to certain parameters and the variables are reduced to a bare minimum. Following on from standard DTL there are now Single-barrel DTL, Handicap-by-distance DTL, and Double-rise, each of which creates its own special problems (these will be dealt with in turn later on). DTL is in fact the easiest and most elementary of the domestic Trap disciplines, being the most commonly found and easily broken of all Trap targets. Most international expert Trap shooters will have gained their first grounding in DTL.

For the beginner gun mount is a major hurdle. As discussed in Chapter 3, tackling targets with the gun already mounted into the shoulder is an ideal initial way of overcoming this problem – indeed, some well-known shooters adopt this mode of operation for the majority of their clay shooting. However, if the shooter wishes to move on and shoot a variety of disciplines, and ultimately live quarry, then it is a bad habit to get into and one which will ultimately cause trouble if rigidly adhered to. Yet for Trap shooting, with all targets disappearing rapidly away from the shooter, shooting gun up is not only desirable but absolutely necessary if maximum scores are to be achieved. For those who shoot little or nothing else – and such shooters do exist – it is not a matter for concern.

THE RULES

The rules for Down-the-Line are contained in CPSA Booklet No. 8 and those for the other Trap disciplines are essentially variations on this central theme. Even the international Trap disciplines have certain similarities in terms of shooter behaviour and squadding.

3.1. Shooting Order
. . . The shooters comprising the squad shall stand at the designated firing marks from 1 to 5 (from left to right facing the trap) in the order in which their names appear on the score card. ALL GUNS SHALL BE OPEN AND EMPTY.

3.2. Shooting DTL
(i)   When all is ready and correct the Referee shall call 'Line Ready'.
(ii)   All competitors may then load two cartridges.
(iii) The first competitor only shall adopt a shooting stance . . . and call 'Pull' or some other word of command.
(iv)   Whereupon the Puller . . . who shall be behind the line of shooters, shall immediately release the target.
(v)   The first shooter may shoot at this target in flight with one or two shots. . . . The resulting score is recorded.

If the competitor scores a 'kill' with the first shot the competitor shall be awarded 3 points, if the competitor scores a 'kill' with the second shot the competitor shall be awarded 2 points. If the competitor fails to 'kill' the target with either shot, the target shall be called 'LOST' and no points shall be awarded . . .

3.3.1.
(i)   Provided that a 'NO BIRD' has not been called and the Referee has announced the result of the shot, the shooter on the second firing mark may then follow the same procedure, followed afterwards by the third shooter and repeated for Nos 4 and 5.
(ii)   . . . Each competitor shall shoot at each firing mark: . . . (d) in a 25 bird stage – 5 targets.

DTL gun mount prior to call – Mayland and District Gun Club

3.3.2.

At such point an audible signal shall be given and the Referee shall call 'change!'. Each shooter (except No.5) then moves to the firing mark next on the right and No. 5 takes the place of No. 1.

3.3.3.

When walking between firing marks each shooter *must* ensure that the gun is open. The shooter leaving No.5 firing mark to take up position at No.1 firing mark must move to that position by walking *behind the line of shooters with the gun open and empty of cartridges or cases.*

3.3.4.

When all is in order . . . the Referee shall call 'Line Ready' and shall do so . . . before the commencement of shooting.

3.3.6.

When all the members of the squad have shot at the required number of targets . . . the Referee shall call 'Unload and check your scores' whereupon *all guns shall be opened and emptied of any cartridges or cases.*

4. Ammunition

As under Rule 3/4 in Chapter 8, English Sporting.

5. Balk

ANY OCCURRENCE WHICH IN THE OPINION OF THE REFEREE MATERIALLY HANDICAPS THE COMPETITOR AFTER THE CALL OF 'PULL', IF IT DETERS THE COMPETITOR FROM SHOOTING OR DISTRACTS AT THE MOMENT OF SHOOTING.

(i)   After any balk the Referee shall declare a 'NO BIRD'.

(ii) Only the competitor directly concerned may claim a 'Balk'.

(iii)   Any claim must be made immediately after the incident in question. Later claims . . . will *not* be permitted.

(iv)   A claim for a 'Balk' which is upheld also constitutes a 'No Bird' and will entitle the competitor to a repeated target.

7. Competitor

A competitor:

(i)   Shall observe the rules . . .

(ii)   Shall shoot and behave in a safe manner at all times.

(iii)   May load only when permitted by the Referee.

(iv)   Is allowed only 15 seconds to call for a target after the result of the preceding shooter's target has been announced by the Referee . . .

(v)   Shall remove any cartridge cases or unfired cartridge from the gun before turning from the firing mark on the cessation of shooting.

(vi)   Shall be at the firing mark within 3 minutes of being DULY NOTIFIED.

(vii)   Shall take sufficient cartridges to complete the stage . . .

(x)   Shall remain at the firing mark until *all* the competitors in the squad have completed the stage.

13. Jury

A JURY OF AT LEAST FIVE COMPETENT PERSONS MAY BE APPOINTED FOR REGISTERED EVENTS.

(c)   The Jury may not overrule a Referee as to whether a target is hit or not.

14. 'Killed' Target

A REGULAR TARGET THAT IN THE OPINION OF THE REFEREE HAS AT LEAST A VISIBLE PIECE BROKEN FROM IT, OR IS COMPLETELY REDUCED TO DUST, OR HAS A VISIBLE PIECE BROKEN FROM IT WHICH IS REDUCED TO DUST, BY THE COMPETITOR'S SHOT.

(i)   A target which has some dust removed from it by the shot but remains otherwise intact is *not* a killed target.

15. Lost Target

(i)   A REGULAR TARGET THAT IS NOT A 'KILLED' TARGET AFTER HAVING BEEN FIRED UPON IN ACCORDANCE WITH THESE RULES.

A target shall be declared 'LOST' when:

(a)   The target remains unbroken after being fired at.

(b)   The competitor after an apparent malfunction or misfire opens the gun or moves the safety catch before handing the gun to the Referee.

(c)   A competitor suffers a 3rd or subsequent malfunction or misfire in the same stage . . .

(d)   An irregular whole target is shot at and missed . . . (Unless the Referee has called 'No Bird' *before or as* the shooter fires the first shot).

(ii)   Or the competitor fails to fire for any reason due to personal fault or negligence.

17. Malfunction (Misfire)

THE REFEREE SHALL ANNOUNCE A MALFUNCTION AND DECLARE A 'NO BIRD' WHERE THERE IS A FAILURE OF A SHOTGUN TO FIRE THE CARTRIDGE DUE TO SOME DEFECT OF THE SHOTGUN MECHANISM.

(a)   (i)   An ammunition defect is not a malfunction.

(ii)   Any cause due to the shooter's fault is not a malfunction . . .

(c)   Second barrel malfunction

An allowable MALFUNCTION on the second shot shall be resolved by:

(i)   the target being declared a 'No Bird'.

(ii)   the competitor shall then repeat the target and the result of the 2nd shot *only* shall be scored.

After calling for the target and its appearance the shooter must fire off the first barrel before firing the second barrel at the target. If the target is killed by the first barrel the target will be declared LOST.

18. Misfire (See Malfunction)

FAILURE OF THE CARTRIDGE TO FIRE OR FUNCTION PROPERLY AFTER THE FIRING PIN HAS MADE PROPER CONTACT WITH THE CARTRIDGE CAP.

THE LAYOUT

DTL layout construction entails few of the problems inherent with Skeet. Strictly speaking there is no need for any permanent set-up, and aside from the small trap house itself a layout could be thrown down on any suitable piece of ground; indeed, the trap house can be of portable construction which gives great flexibility. This is all well and good for the smaller operation, such as a local club using a non-electric trap, but for Registered DTL the layouts need to be precisely set out, although even then complete permanence of the trap house is not absolutely necessary. It is not uncommon for DTL and the closely related Automatic Ball Trap (ABT) to utilise the same layout. Where this occurs a movable DTL trap house is essential. The size of the trap house needs some attention, for it determines the precise moment at which a fleeing target is first seen. The CPSA recommends certain

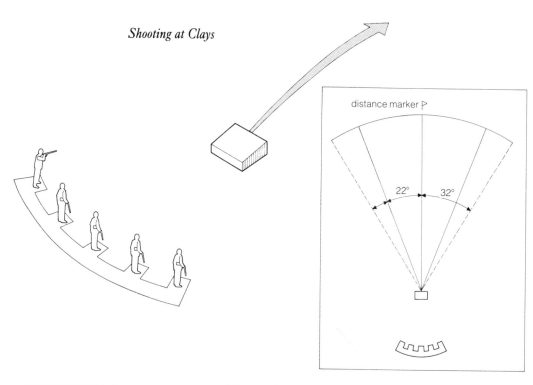

distance marker ▷

22° 32°

Figure 22 Standard
DTL layout

measurements, as follows: the height of the trap house is of particular importance and should be within 4 inches (0.1 m) plus or minus of the prescribed 2 feet 6 inches (0.76 m); the width should be within 6 inches (0.16 m) either side of 8 feet (2.44 m), with the same recommended dimension for the trap-house length. Ideally all trap houses should conform to these dimensions, to ensure that targets are never seen that split-second earlier from one layout to another.

The parameters within which a DTL layout must be set out are fulfilled easily enough, the basic requirements being as follows:

(a) The trap base must be on the same level as the stands accommodating the shooters.
(b) There must be five stands, one for each shooter.
(c) The stands must be on a reasonably flat area measuring 3 feet by 3 feet (91 cm by 91 cm).
(d) Each of the five stands should be placed 16 yards (14.63 m) behind the trap, with the centre of the centre stand (number 3) in line with a straight away target fired from a zeroed trap; this will have the effect of giving an arc from which the shooters operate.
(e) Each of the five stands must be 9 feet (2.74 m) apart.

The accompanying drawing shows just how simple the DTL layout really is.

The target landing areas are less rigidly defined than with Skeet, but none the less there are limits within which the targets must fall. The targets must not travel further than 55 yards (50.3 m) nor less than 50 yards (45.7 m), and it is common practice for a marker peg to be positioned down-range, taking a line from the centre of stand 3 through the trap arm to the required distance. The peg may be set at either of the distances stipulated above, with the minimum marker perhaps the most usual. Two further markers should be present, these being the angle markers to take account of the fact that target angles will vary within prescribed limits; maximum angles are normally shown – these being 32 degrees either side of the centre line – although targets will mostly be thrown well inside this maximum and are more likely to conform to 22 degrees either side of the centre line.

As with Skeet, height of target is a crucial consideration. For DTL the target at a point 30 feet (9.14 m) from the trap shall have attained a height of no less than 8 feet (2.44 m) and no more than 10 feet (3.05 m). The trap will almost certainly need adjustment from one shoot to another to take account of varying wind direction and speed, and providing that the height is right everything else should fall into place. Thus, an ostensibly repetitious and easy target can be seen to have a fair degree of in-built variation; this may be as much as 2 feet (0.6 m) on the height, and 5 yards (4.52 m) at the distance marker, with variation in angles of as much as 32 degrees either side of centre – a difference of as much as 56 yards (51.2 m) at the extremes of angle. It is a far cry from the easy going-away target referred to at the beginning of this chapter.

EQUIPMENT

Target presentation

The actual targets will be standard-sized and invariably, according to background, either orange or yellow; such targets are frequently referred to as 'blaze', a term which may cover a wide spread of targets, with actual coloration varying from one manufacturer to another. The use of black targets for Registered competitions is widely frowned upon – quite rightly so in my view: a black target cannot be seen quite as quickly as an orange one as it leaves the trap house and as a result scores can be adversely affected. The hardness of targets is something else which can vary a good deal depending on manufacture; with DTL the softer the target the better, and really there can be no excuse for using in DTL the sort of hard targets often used in the Trench disciplines. DTL targets rather flop off the trap arm so that very little shock is imparted to the departing target; therefore there is less likelihood of a break at launch, and this makes it possible for the shoot organiser to choose a good reliable target which will not shatter on launch, yet will break satisfactorily when hit. The sort of top-class scores needed to achieve success at DTL are hard enough to accumulate at the best of times without having to contend with hard targets.

The targets will be distributed in a completely random manner within the parameters set out above, using a trap designed for such a purpose. Fortunately, the days are long gone when target variation relied on the judgement of the trapper in varying the target position on the trap arm; neither is it any longer possible for the astute shooter who understood trap mechanisms to calculate at what angle the next target would appear (although there were perhaps relatively few capable of such gamesmanship). These days a wide range of electric traps exists, most of which utilise a 240-volt power supply, and these tend to use far more efficient methods of varying target presentation; as it is vital that random target presentation is completely unpredictable, all the best traps oscillate but also have built-in interruptors. The Winchester White Flyer is one of the most effective and popular of DTL traps; it is an automatic cocking trap, with electric release but manual loading. Therefore, typically with this type of trap, the arm is constantly moving from left to right and back again, and with the cycle interrupted at irregular intervals it is quite impossible to predict just which type of target will come next. Fully automatic traps are becoming increasingly popular, especially with the gun clubs, who are thereby saved the time and expense of trappers. These large magazine-fed traps, such as the Farey, are highly regarded for target presentation and consistency. So long as the magazines are carefully loaded to avoid cracking the targets, there should be few problems, although possibly there may be a slightly higher incidence of broken targets at launch due to the machine's inability to recognise a cracked or chipped clay. This is a factor which must be taken into account when choosing between manual and automatic loading.

Consistency of both target flight and release is crucial in this discipline. Once the targets have been set for the day there should be little variation other than if the weather conditions alter: the target will rise through its specified height, reach a maximum elevation and thereafter begin its descent to land within the specified distance. However, changes in prevailing weather conditions can play havoc with scores: a following wind can flatten DTL targets to an extraordinary degree; conversely an in-coming wind will cause the targets to continue rising remorselessly. Both these factors can be taken account of in trap adjustment if the wind remains consistent, but this is seldom the case, with the almost inevitable gusts causing targets to perform erratically in flight. The problem is made worse by the relatively slow flight of the DTL target, and there is, of course, no way round it other than postponing the shoot in hopes of a day with more favourable conditions. DTL shooters must, of course, grit their teeth and get on with the job in hand, hoping that other competitors get most of the erratic targets.

Button release is excellent on modern traps, but unfortunately it is only as good as its operator. Inconsistencies can occur, and when they do it is the right of the shooter to refuse the target and expect another which conforms to Rule 24: 'A person . . . shall release targets . . . immediately after the shooter's call.' In this context, 'immediately' means exactly that. The acoustic release mechanisms referred to in the chapters dealing with other Trap disciplines are an excellent way of ensuring that such inconsistencies do not creep in; however, these cost in excess of £500 per layout to install and few DTL clubs can justify this sort of expenditure unless they also run ABT or Trench.

Ammunition, guns and miscellanea

Choice of DTL shooting hardware is of crucial importance, particularly cartridge shot sizes and the degree of barrel choking.

In no other clay-pigeon discipline (apart from Double-rise DTL) is points-scoring a feature, but with DTL there is an award for first-barrel kills (three points) and second-barrel kills (two points); so although two shots are allowed for each target it is the first shot which really piles up the points, and it is therefore vital that the maximum possible number of first-barrel kills is achieved. Competition scoring will therefore be over the number of targets (a hundred for all big shoots), with the maximum number of points 300; it will be the competitor with the highest points total who ultimately wins, and while 100-straight at DTL is not uncommon the maximum 100/300 most certainly is. DTL shooters therefore gear themselves up to break each target with the first shot – although they are happy enough to accept two points as an alternative to a lost target.

'Trap cartridge' is perhaps one of the most sweeping and misleading of terms to be found in the shooting world. An individual shooter's perception of what constitutes 'Trap' may differ considerably from another's, and in extreme cases this may be any type of cartridge not widely used in the field. To the clay shooter there can be no doubting just what a Trap cartridge really is, although the diversity and variety on offer may cause a good deal of initial confusion for the beginner. As with Skeet, there is precious little to choose between the better-known brands; there are similarities in appearance, price and indeed in performance, so that actual choice is often largely a matter of individual preference, not necessarily based on anything precise. Individual bias based on a whole range of factors may determine choice for some, while the saving of a pound or two on a purchase of perhaps 1000 cartridges may make all the difference to others.

Unquestionably some loads do match individual guns better than others, but invariably there will be next to nothing to choose between brands. Very often, once a shooter has settled on a gun/cartridge combination which suits him, he will be loath to change. Spoilt for choice is an apt phrase when considering Trap loads, and this is compounded by the propensity of cartridge manufacturers constantly to produce new (and supposedly improved) loads. However, in all fairness the development of products referred to in the chapter dealing with English Skeet affects Trap equally, and does much to benefit the shooting community. Thus today we find some very fast Trap loads which pattern well and deliver a telling punch at good range without knocking over the shooter every time a shot is fired.

The standard trap load will usually consist of 1 oz of shot packed into a plastic cup wad to protect the pellets from excessive deformity caused by contact with the barrel, a plastic case as protection against the elements, backed up by a powder which burns both quickly and cleanly. The shooter can ask for little more. The standard load will thus do all that is asked of it, and most shooters will be satisfied with this. However, also freely available is a range of upgraded cartridges capable of packing that extra punch at the longer ranges which can be encountered on the DTL range, and these are especially useful for second-barrel kills after an initial miss. Whether there is any real gain in using such punchy and more expensive loads is a matter of personal opinion. Further up the scale come the much more expensive nickel loads, which may also be seen on the DTL range from time to time. They are really designed for use on the faster ABT and Trench targets – but there is no impediment to using them against DTL, and without question they can produce some quite devastating long-range kills.

By way of example, before the advent of 1 oz loads Winchester produced their wonderful range of Trap loads; the Trap 100 was very much the standard load; the Trap 200 was the cartridge with more devastating killing power, suitable for both DTL and the higher Trap disciplines; finally, the Trap 300 was the nickel load designed for the destruction of long-range Trench targets. Other manufacturers worked along similar lines, with Maionchi and Eley further examples – all good competition loads with little to separate them in terms of performance and cost.

Although the rules for DTL clearly state that the maximum shot size permissible is number 6 English with a maximum shot load of 1 oz, in practice 7½s are most widely used. This size of pellet will pattern well – dependent on choke – while still retaining sufficient striking energy to break targets at maximum ranges. Number 8 shot is fairly popular, particularly as a first-barrel load when the target is at its closest, and the slightly higher pellet count can often give the chippy kill where a miss might otherwise occur. This is very much a matter of individual choice, and among the top shooters there will be a good cross-section demonstrating the case for just about every combination imaginable.

As explained earlier, it is fair to say that any flat-shooting field gun can be used against any clay discipline with remarkably good effect. Yet if there were ever a clear case of horses for courses then it is here: it is an absolute necessity to use a proper Trap gun for tackling DTL on a regular basis. The right gun will make it so much easier to break targets consistently, although there may well be an initial traumatic period of adjustment.

The Trap guns used by DTL shooters are basically heavy, high-shooting, long-barrelled, tightly-choked weapons. Barrels of 30 inches are the norm, with an increasing tendency towards using 32-inch versions. The extra weight inherent in long-barrelled guns is a valuable asset for the Trap shooter; recoil is greatly absorbed, which is an especially important point as the necessary gun-up stance can sometimes exacerbate the problems caused by recoil. The reduction of recoil is also beneficial in the reduction of discernible muzzle-flip at the first shot, which is particularly important when retaining a steady sight picture for taking second-barrel shots. Equally important, long heavy barrels slow down the shooter, making him steadier and less likely to flip the muzzles over the rising target – one of the most common causes of missing for even the experienced Trap shooter.

The raised comb (top of the stock) on Trap guns lifts the shooter's head and in effect creates a sight picture whereby a fair amount of top rib is visible. This sight picture will vary greatly from one manufacturer to another; some Trap guns shoot fairly flat while others have a very high comb and consequently place the shot very high. It is a question of individual preference, and it is not possible to state categorically that one height of comb has any advantage over another. The net effect of the sight picture is that the target remains visible at all times, and the shooter has to fire low in order to achieve a kill. How low will, of course, depend on the height of comb. Some Trap guns perform best with the target sitting virtually on top of the foresight while others may need several inches of daylight between foresight and target. Although a flat-shooting gun can suffice, because it actually blots out the target any shooter thus equipped is likely to find himself at a disadvantage – especially where a second-barrel shot is needed to finish the job.

Most certainly the majority of Trap guns now conform to a clearly defined format: over-and-under, with a raised ventilated rib; single-trigger; non-returnable safety catch; automatic ejectors; padded butt plates, and often a palm swell on the neck of the stock. The ventilated rib is an important part of the gun rather than a cosmetic feature, for it helps to keep the barrels cool, as does a ventilated centre rib. Wide top ribs help to dissipate the inevitable heat haze which forms around the muzzle so that it is less noticeable to the shooter as he prepares for the next target, and the step-rib seen on many modern Trap guns fulfils a similar function. Other types of gun are now rarely seen in DTL, although Trap semi-automatics were quite popular at one time; as with all semi-autos, their relative lack of recoil made them a good choice for anyone not happy with constant and repetitive heavy recoil. Now they are most definitely out of fashion. Where a semi-auto is used it must be modified so that the ejected case does not interfere with the shooter standing next in line – on the right for a right-hand-ejecting semi-auto.

The most appropriate degree of choke for DTL is also very much a matter for individual preference, although the majority of Trap guns come with very tight borings. My own Trap gun has ¾ and Full and is far too tight for slow DTL targets, which are essentially taken close in – less than 30 yards in the main – when the need is for width as opposed to density of pattern. Many years ago when I used a semi-auto I used ½ choke, and this was a good compromise in a single-barrel gun; ½ choke is quite adequate for even the longest of DTL targets – especially when one considers the not inconsiderable killing power of modern cartridges – and from this it is possible to decide on choking in a double-barrel over-and-under. The tendency towards over-tight chokings is undoubtedly due to the manufacturers producing guns for the wider Trap-shooting market.

A Trap gun is almost certainly not designed for exclusive DTL work – there is a huge market available elsewhere in Europe among shooters whose taste is for the more demanding Trench disciplines – and when one begins to consider ABT and Trench then the need for tighter chokes becomes more readily apparent. If the shooter wishes to flit from one Trap discipline to another, he will probably have to settle for a compromise; pure adherence to the DTL discipline can allow a greater refinement.

For me the optimum choking will be either ½ and ¾, or ¼ and ½. Many shooters prefer the former as this will still not rule out tackling those more demanding Trap disciplines. Some Trap guns are available with interchangeable choke tubes. Most frequently it will be the bottom barrel only which has this valuable facility; as this is the barrel which fires the first shot every time and is responsible for the highest percentage of kills, this formula is probably about right. Obviously a changeable choke facility will have an upward effect on the price of a gun, but it may well be a worthwhile item of expenditure. For the purest DTL shooter who wants the sort of open choking referred to, the choice is simply one of ordering a gun with such chokes specified, or else having the choking opened out by a reputable gunsmith. If there is one overriding drawback to having the choking taken out, it is that this is an irreversible operation and therefore one should consider carefully before proceeding.

Other items of equipment for DTL shooters do not differ radically from those pertaining to other clay shooters. However, among Trap

Typical trap shooter's gun rest position (on this occasion a Trench shooter)

shooters in general there seems to be a greater tendency to wear the clay shooter's 'uniform' of blue Skeet vest, trainer shoes with muzzle pad attached to the appropriate foot, peaked cap and tinted glasses. The peaked cap acts as an excellent foil against the bright glare of sky above the shooting range, while the tinted glasses fulfil a similar function; the muzzle pad is important, as a Trap gun is a heavy object which spends most of its working life open awaiting the next shot, so it needs resting somewhere – as the photograph demonstrates. Muzzle pads save either ruined footwear due to black muzzle-rings, or else damaged gun barrels due to constant contact with the ground. A further notable item of equipment are the blinkers worn by many shooters; these are usually derived from torn-up cartridge boxes slid on to the shaft of glasses; they are a very helpful aid to concentration as they blot out any movement going on round about.

Typical trap shooter's gun rest position (on this occasion a Trench shooter)

TECHNIQUE

Procedure

DTL shooting consists of a five-man squad present on the layout, with each shooter taking up his allotted position; from this position each shooter is presented with five targets, which are shot one at a time moving from left to right along the line. After five targets have been completed each shooter moves one place to the right, the shooter on stand 5 moving behind the line to take up the new position on stand 1. This procedure is repeated until each shooter in the squad has shot at five targets from each of the five stands, thus completing twenty-five

Narrow
sideways-on DTL
stance – Kent
Wildfowlers
ground

targets in all. The shooter will thus be confronted with a surprisingly wide range of target angles, which will vary from straight-away to sharp left-hander or sharp right-hander and, of course, all the lesser angles in between. As explained earlier, the oscillating trap ensures that there is no possibility of pre-judging the exact line of flight of any target and this means that the shooter needs to adopt a technique capable of tackling this variety of angles without undue discomfort. Various refinements of technique exist amongst DTL shooters, although these are in fact merely variations on a central theme; a brief examination of the most commonly used techniques will therefore guide the emergent DTL shooter, subsequent adaptation to suit personal needs being part of the shooter's evolutionary process.

Stance
The simple rules relating to stance, as cited in earlier chapters dealing with Sporting and Skeet, cannot really apply to DTL: with a target of varying angles it is not possible to stand precisely to address the expected point of contact with the target, and the shooter will need to adopt the sort of stance which is essentially a compromise. Most DTL shooters stand almost sideways on to the expected line of flight – as in the photograph – so that they are capable of relatively easy movement from right to left, and vice versa. Inevitably there will be variations,

some favouring a more open stance with the chest facing the trap house more than in the illustration. Most shooters prefer a fairly upright stance, with the feet no more than a foot apart and the weight thrown forward on to the front foot; others may adopt a more squat stance, although this is fairly uncommon among top-class DTL shooters. The emergent DTL shooter should, however, guard against standing rigidly erect, as this may have the effect of sending the shot high above the target. This will apply doubly to any second shot being taken, so it is important to lean into the gun sufficiently to maintain position for that second shot. Once the correct stance has been sorted out, it is time to consider the target in more detail.

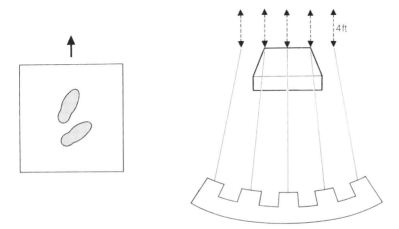

Shooting DTL

The shooter does not know the line of flight, which is the variable, but he does know that every target will be flying away from him and climbing at the same time; hence the essential gun-up mode of the Trap shooter. As the line drawing demonstrates, there is a range of gun-hold positions which the shooter will need to adopt and these will vary according to which stand the shooter happens to be on at the time and, of course, from one shooter to another. Height of gun hold varies greatly from one shooter to another – indeed, the same shooter may vary that hold position depending on prevailing conditions; whichever height is opted for, there are various factors both for and against. A low hold position on or even slightly below the front lip of the trap house gives the shooter the advantage of seeing the target instantly no matter what its line of flight; on the debit side, there may be a very real danger of lifting the muzzles too swiftly, which often results in a miss over the top of the target. A higher hold position – anything up to 4 feet depending on the shooter concerned – will have the not inconsiderable advantage of needing little more than lateral movement of the gun to

Figure 23
Down-the-Line –
feet and gun hold
positions

get on to the target; however, there are occasions when the target sneaks out from under the raised barrels unobserved until the last moment; this can sometimes cause momentary panic in the inexperienced shooter. As with so much in DTL it is often a case of striking the best compromise, and the fact that so many shooters turn in remarkably high scores testifies that it is a problem which is far from insurmountable.

It cannot be denied that DTL, by its very nature, is unfair in that there is no even spread of targets among the squad and, because of the continual and uncontrolled oscillation of the trap, there is no way that such a spread can be achieved. Nevertheless this is part and parcel of shooting DTL, and the totally random presentation of targets is one of the necessary methods of testing the shooter. It may work out that the same shooter gets a high proportion of straight or shallow-angled targets, while a competitor on the same squad gets a preponderance of sharp angles. Among top DTL shooters, however, there is not necessarily a direct correlation between sharp-angled targets and lower scores, for provided technique is sound each type of target should be dealt with equally efficiently. A common enough mistake among beginners is the tendency to try to prejudge where the next target is going to fly; it is quite impossible to do so accurately, although it may be difficult to overcome the subconscious which says, 'That last target was a sharp left-hander, therefore this one won't be.' All too often it is, and the shooter may be a fraction late in responding, which will often have the net effect of his frantically and hopelessly chasing an escaping target. It is far better to treat each target as it comes, armed with the knowledge that it really can do anything.

Watching the previous shooter's targets can be a fatal fascination. It can encourage too much consideration of potential flight path. To avoid distraction some shooters stare fixedly at the ground although this approach does take a great deal of discipline and can be upset by the slightest interruption to routine. It is far more common to see top shooters gazing blissfully out over the trap house so as to remain aware of the preceding target without being fixated by it. This latter method is of particular use early on in a squad when weather conditions are variable, as it gives the shooter the opportunity of watching for any variation in target: the target which climbs remorselessly into a head wind, or the flattening target being buffeted by a following wind may need different treatment, and the astute shooter will quickly work this out. Perhaps the overriding rule for all DTL shooting is to shoot the targets as quickly as technique and circumstances allow; in this way the target which conforms to the set height, as all should irrespective of weather conditions, can be dealt with before the wind has had its insidious effect. It is easier said than done perhaps, but a style well worth cultivating.

Stand 1

For this stand most shooters adopt a gun-hold position outside the left-hand edge of the trap house. How far depends on the individual, but 1–3 feet should cover most eventualities. On this stand, and on stand 5, the shooter is likely to come across the sharpest-angled targets on the layout. Seen from stand 3, the centre, the same target seems innocuous enough, but on stand 1 it becomes a fast left-hander which the shooter must get on to swiftly if it is not to beat him for speed. It is probably fair to say that few DTL shooters have any conception of lead *per se*, but on this stand the sharp left-handed target will need lead of a couple of feet or more if it is to be broken. On this stand, as indeed on every other, it is the straight-away target (the sharp right-hander to the shooter when on stand 5) which can cause problems and the shooter will have to guard against the two main reasons for missing – swinging back too far and missing down the right-hand side, and missing over the top. Similarly, the various quartering angles in between those described will all pose their own problems. Each one will require a certain amount of lead, the lead being seen as a shot fired down the left-hand side of the target.

Stand 2

Because the shooter has changed position, moving in towards the centre, the angles have been reduced; the violent left-hand target has disappeared, but in its stead we find some deceptive shallow angles on which the shooter must concentrate fully. For this stand the gun-hold position should be around the extreme left-hand edge of the trap house. This will allow the shooter to pick out the left-hander quickly, while also allowing plenty of opportunity to come back for the straight and right-hand targets without too much difficulty. On this stand perception of lead is much reduced, with most targets requiring no more than a minimal amount of 'side'; invariably a shot fired a few inches down the side of the angled target will suffice, but the shooter must guard against pointing and stopping the swing – a certain recipe for missing – even though it may seem hard to get much swing going when moving the muzzle so little.

Stand 3

The centre stand and arguably the easiest on the layout. Strictly speaking no targets should ever be missed on this stand, simply because the angles are only slight variations on the straight-away target and therefore easily dealt with by the minimum of gun movement. In practice, of course, it is another matter, and if the shooter starts to think that here are the really easy targets, a miss may well occur. Gun-hold position should be about centre, although some shooters favour a position just to one side of the centre – to either the left or right.

Stand 4
The shooter has now moved right of centre, and finds an exact reversal of the situation encountered on stand 2: the angles are shallow, but maximum concentration is required, especially if the scoring thus far has been good. Gun-hold position needs to be on the right-hand edge of the trap house to take account of the right-hander, but as specified under Stand 2, little in the way of lead is needed.

Stand 5
The last stand and a reversal of the potential problems encountered on stand 1. Gun-hold position needs to be to the right-hand side of the trap house, again 1–3 feet depending on technique. For the right-hand Shot this right-hand target can be a brute to deal with and often seems to have picked up extra speed into the bargain; of course this is not so, rather that the shooter is gaining a truer perception of the real speed of DTL targets when shooting from stands 1 and 5. Concentration is, as ever with DTL, the key and a fast yet smooth response to the right-hander will yield success. The vagaries of DTL being what they are, it is quite possible to shoot all five targets from this stand without receiving a single sharp-angled target; conversely, almost every target can be of this description, and this knowledge should be enough to remind the shooter to keep an open mind.

If the shooter has concentrated and worked hard he will have come off with a 25-straight which may or may not include some second-barrel kills; the ultimate goal is the perfect 25/75, which repeated fourfold will almost certainly win most competitions. The mental challenge and the sneaky angles of DTL ensure that 100/300 is sufficiently rare to remain notable, and no amount of criticism in some quarters of 'boring' DTL can alter the fact that it takes a very good Shot indeed to achieve that perfect tally.

HIGH STANDARDS

DTL is immensely popular in Britain today and since there is no substitute for practice, it is perhaps stating the obvious to say that the top shooters do shoot an enormous number of targets, several thousand per annum per shooter being commonplace. National team selection procedures – which are discussed in Chapter 15 – dictate that the successful qualifiers have to shoot many times to gain recognition. Selection shoots at other disciplines may seem expensive at first glance, but invariably national honours are far more expensive to acquire for the DTL shooter who has even more selection shoots to choose from. Some idea of the enormous dedication and cost involved in acquiring an England team place can be formulated by a glance through the CPSA Members' Averages book. This shows that Paul

Ward shot 8700 Registered DTL targets during the 1989/90 period for an astonishingly high average of 97.7 per cent – A/A class. In the ladies, M. Rowley shot 6450 targets for an average of 91.6 per cent – A class. Extraordinary dedication is the hallmark of the DTL shooter, with high averages not easily retained over a twelve-month period.

A number of DTL variants also exist and are shot on a county, regional and national competitive basis. Double-rise, Single-barrel and Handicap-by-distance DTL are all practised with varying degrees of enthusiasm. None of these, it seems, will ever attain a truly widespread following, although of the three Double-rise is fairly popular.

DOUBLE-RISE

As the name implies, Double-rise is in essence DTL with two targets thrown simultaneously. There is no target variation as there is with the single target, both targets being set up to fly the same each time; in fact there is no need to have varying targets, for the presentation of two targets at once is quite enough of a challenge for most shooters to be going on with. The same DTL layout is used, with the same trap and ancillaries, the only changes being a few alterations to the trap in order for it to accommodate the throwing of two targets. Trap alterations involve the necessary adjustment to prevent oscillating; increased elevation in order to make the targets sit up higher; and increased tension on the spring to make the targets carry further. When setting up a Double-rise layout the aim should be for both targets to fly at equal angles either side of the centre line – ideally within 37 degrees either side of the centre – while at the same time ensuring that the targets fly the regulation distance and are presented at a reasonable height. Invariably Double-rise targets consist of one target which flies nicely on a regular trajectory while the other tends to curl away slightly; this can be overcome to some extent by setting the targets to fly fairly high, but Double-rise shooters are wise enough to expect this curling target as part and parcel of the discipline. A good rule of thumb is that the angled target should appear as a straight-away target from stations 1 and 5 respectively; if it does, the shooter knows that the pair on offer are just about right.

Equipment is the same as for DTL. With Double-rise there is a better than ever case for using number 8 shot in the first barrel, followed by 7½s for the second shot, for there will be no surprises in store and no sharp angles for which the shooter is not ready. Because every pair will be the same the shooter can forget about variations in target flight and concentrate on technique – which is the deciding factor in Double-rise more than any other.

Unquestionably it should be a relatively easy matter to break the first

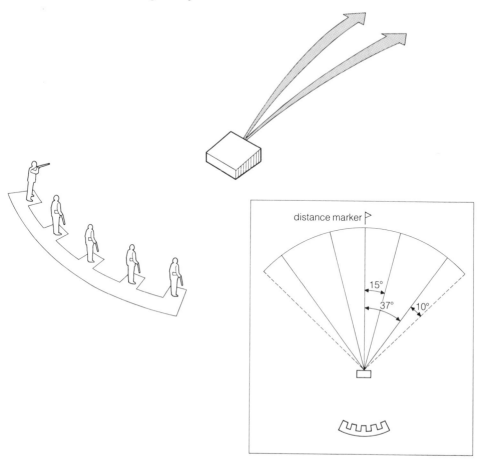

Figure 24
Double-rise – note
the wider angles

target of each pair, but the second is a much harder proposition. This is recognised in the scoring, which allows five points for a pair of targets; all competitions are over a certain number of pairs for which points are awarded on the basis of five for a pair and two for a single, with nothing, of course, for a double miss. Both targets must be fired at in turn, so that there is no possibility of firing two shots at the same target in order to get at least some points in the bag. Thus for fifty pairs the maximum score is 250 points, and it is a very accomplished Double-rise shooter who gets anywhere near that. The art in Double-rise is to establish a rhythm of breaking pairs consistently, for with the loss of three points for every single missed target it does not take long to fall irretrievably behind.

TECHNIQUE

Technique really is crucial with this discipline, and it is not necessarily the best DTL Shots who produce the best Double-rise points totals.

The decision about which target to take first is a vitally important one, and the shooter must reach an early decision and stick to it; swapping about haphazardly from one target to the other will only bring about ultimate confusion and end with a string of misses. Once the decision has been made the first target should be addressed in positive fashion. Because the line of flight is known it may suit the shooter to hold a higher than normal gun position for what should be an easy target. The top Double-rise shooter will seldom if ever miss his first target, relying on this as his 'banker' and thereafter using his smooth precise technique to pick out the second target.

The shooter will have to adopt one of two tactics in order to deal with a testing combination of targets. There are basically two systems in use: firstly, to shoot one target first all the way through a round, irrespective of which station the shooter happens to be on at the time; secondly, the shooter may decide always to shoot the straight-away target first, and this will, of course, vary according to shooting station. Many right-handed shooters go for the right-hand target first each time, swinging back left-handed for the second target. This technique offers target combinations of varying difficulty, with, on station 1, a straight-away target first followed by a sharp left-hander; the angles will alter relative to the station position until on station 5 the shooter is confronted with a right-hander which swings quickly across him from left to right, with the second target straight away to the left. In each case the shooter will know the flight of target with a degree of precision and should thus be able to pick up the target with ease, even when it is the sharp right-hander, thereby leaving himself plenty of time for the second target. The shooter who opts for the left target first will, of course, find the situation in reverse. This technique is perhaps as good as any, and so long as the shooter is careful in establishing a rhythm there should be few problems.

Those who favour shooting the straighter of the two targets first may experience fewer problems with angles, the straight target offering fewer problems than the angled targets encountered in the system first described. The main drawback is that on stations 1 and 2 the shooter has to swing back left-handed for the second target; on stations 4 and 5 he has to come back right-handed for the second target. Station 3 offers a pair of targets both of which are in essence evenly spread, thus offering the shooter a choice; because at Double-rise one of the targets almost always falls away quickly, this is usually the target to take first. So long as the shooter can swing comfortably both left-handed and right-handed, this system is perhaps the one to adopt.

Actual gun-hold position is important, as indeed it is with DTL, although with Double-rise it is possible to hold rather higher than normal; this allows the first target to be taken very quickly, leaving plenty of time to swing across for the second shot. However, this should never be overdone, since any excessive rushing is bound to result in a missed first target. Throughout the shooter's apprenticeship at Double-rise one overriding factor should be borne in mind – there is plenty of time for a smooth, calculating shooting style to have maximum effect. The best Double-rise shots always seem to be so quick and precise, coming back for the second target as it levels out; this is perhaps the key to the whole exercise, for the majority of shooters will find the second target beginning to fall by the time they are able to fire. The ability to hit a falling target does not come easily, the muzzles being forced through and below the target in order to achieve a hit. As with all facets of clay shooting, practice is the key. The comparative dearth of Double-rise availability undoubtedly causes a problem here. The habit of many DTL shooters of shooting at pieces of broken clay is not bravado but a means of staying sharp and accurate. It serves as useful practice, and is probably as near to shooting at irregular DTL targets as most shooters can get.

More than any other Trap discipline, Double-rise is about technique and timing rather than about actual Trap-shooting skill. It is a discipline well suited to the sort of all-round skills often displayed by Sporting shooters, and it is no coincidence that the major Double-rise championships are not always won by Trap shooters. The popularity of the discipline's major championships speaks volumes for the sport, although the fact that traditionally the British Double-rise Championship is among the first of the big national championships of the year – being held in March – may well have an effect on entries. Championship-starved clay shooters after the winter lay-off are apt to shoot at anything during the opening weeks of the season, although this is not something which should detract from the spectacle of the event or from the undoubted achievement in winning.

SINGLE-BARREL DTL

Shooting Single-barrel DTL is about shooting at standard DTL targets with one cartridge only loaded, not shooting DTL with a single-barrel gun. In every way this discipline conforms to the same criteria used for DTL, and should be no great challenge to shooters capable of hitting almost 100 per cent of their DTL targets with the first shot under normal circumstances. It is the form of DTL most common in the United States, where it is enormously popular. Yet Single-barrel DTL has never been widely popular in Great Britain, and with standard DTL so deeply entrenched it is not very likely that there will be any upsurge in interest in what is essentially a spin-off.

In terms of technique, Single-barrel DTL makes no extra demands on the shooter. However, there is a certain mental problem which can strike at the regular DTL shooter with devastating results – and as with Double-rise there is not the competitive practice available to ensure any degree of consistency. Shorn of the security of that second shot, the DTL shooter can become curiously inhibited and uncertain, and it is quite common for the shooter to hang on the target in an attempt to make sure. As stated many times in these pages, if there is one certain road to disaster in clay shooting then it is to hesitate even momentarily before pulling the trigger. Successful Single-barrel DTL shooters treat the target with the sort of disdain normally reserved for the more traditional offering, and in this way often power their way to a big score. Near-maximum scores often win the major championships, with 95/100 or more almost guaranteed to be rewarded with a placing at any shoot.

HANDICAP-BY-DISTANCE DTL

Of all the DTL variants this is undoubtedly the least widespread, really appearing on a regular basis only in the national championships. It is a mutant form of DTL supposedly designed to even out the difference in the classes by placing those in the lowest class nearest to the trap, with each class being placed successively further away until the highest class (A/A) is standing at the maximum distance. Whether or not the technique works as a leveller is open to doubt, as the top shooters invariably come through as usual; it does, however, create a degree of interest and is a harmless and enjoyable change from the normal run-of-the-mill DTL.

The dividing lines between the classes compare with the normal 16 yards are as follows:

Class A/A: 23 yards behind the trap
Class A: 21 yards behind the trap
Class B: 19 yards behind the trap
Class C: 17 yards behind the trap

Obviously classes are squadded together, so there is no chance of dangerous mayhem being created by the mixing of the classes within squads. Techniques are broadly similar to those in standard DTL, with the class C shooter scarcely noticing any difference. However, when the shooter gets out to the class A or A/A distances, the targets become progressively more demanding. Even the quickest shooter is going to find himself confronted with a target in the order of 40 yards for the first shot, while angles will become noticeably different. The extra ranges encountered by the upper-class shooters effectively discourage the use of the smaller number 8 shot size, and most shooters will be well advised to stick to 7½s once they have graduated to the 21 and 23 yards distances. This is a challenging variation, although not one which at present seems likely to catch on at local level.

13 Automatic Ball Trap

Automatic Ball Trap (ABT), known more commonly as Ball Trap, is the first of the international Trap disciplines to be considered in this book and features here because of certain similarities with DTL. It is generally considered to be a more difficult form of DTL, and is often used as a training ground for the more demanding Trench disciplines described in the next two chapters. Although it is much more demanding than DTL, it is still considered less than favourably by most Trench shooters because of what they perceive as its inherent unfairnesses. None the less there are certain close interrelations between the four Trap disciplines: frequently the trap used is of the DTL/ABT type, which can easily be converted from one discipline to the other after a few basic and easy adjustments; and Trench layouts can often be utilised for ABT, once again with no more than a few minor adjustments – indeed, it is not unusual to find a single Trap layout marked up for the different disciplines, which ensures that costly duplication of layout does not occur unless it is unavoidable.

The rules for Automatic Ball Trap are contained in CPSA Booklet No. 11, and are recommended reading for any shooter contemplating taking up ABT on a regular basis.

THE LAYOUT

ABT targets, in common with the other international Trap disciplines, are thrown from below ground level; thereafter they quickly attain the prescribed height and are set to travel the required minimum distance. Just as with DTL, the shooting stations are in an arc behind the trap house, although there the similarities end. The trap house must be constructed so that the top of the roof – usually the front – is on a level with the shooting stations; the front of the shooting station is situated 49 feet 2 inches (15 m) to the rear of the front of the trap house; the shooting station itself is 3 feet 3 inches (1 m) square, with 9 feet 10 inches (3 m) between the front centre of each shooting station. This creates an arc of five shooting stations, as it does with DTL. There is no definitive stipulation regarding the size of the trap house roof, although the recommendation is for a width of approximately 13 feet

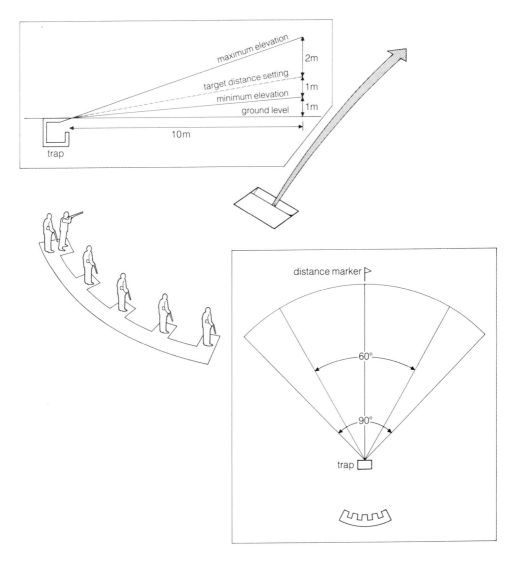

Figure 25 Automatic
Ball Trap layout

(4 m) and a depth of 6 feet 6 inches (2 m). Ideally the trap-house roof should be level with the ground, in which case the clay will always appear out of the ground rather than out of the side of a built-up layout, something which occurs from time to time. In this way there is no advantage – no matter how minute – for any shooter on the line. The height from floor to roof of the trap house pit may vary, but for maximum storage space and ease of use 6 feet 6 inches (2 m) is recommended.

ABT targets differ from DTL in terms of greater speed, wider angles and variable heights. At a height of 6 feet 6 inches (2 m), measured 32 feet 6 inches (10 m) forward of the trap house, the target should attain the maximum permitted distance of 246 feet (75 m), with a plus or minus variation of 15 feet 3 inches (5 m). It can be seen that the ABT target is much faster than its DTL counterpart, travelling some 50 per cent further. Variations on elevation will naturally affect target carrying distance and therefore target speed over the full range of its flight; however, initial speeds will not vary, although as angles and heights vary the shooter's perception of speed may alter radically. Using the front edge of the trap house roof as the datum, the height of the target should not vary beyond a minimum of 3 feet 3 inches (1 m) and a maximum of 13 feet (4 m). The varied angles will also be much wider than can be found legally on the DTL layout; as the line drawing shows, the minimum permissible angle is 60 degrees, the maximum 90 degrees. It can be seen that the range of targets on offer to the ABT shooter is varied and challenging, with almost every imaginable permutation available at random.

EQUIPMENT

The trap is electrically operated, whether loaded automatically or by hand; it has two multi-oscillating electric motors complete with interruptors, one motor to control angles, the second to control elevations. Such traps are substantial and expensive pieces of equipment, although the actual functioning side is fairly basic. This type of trap throws targets in a completely random manner. The targets themselves are frequently orange, but may be any colour which will be readily seen against the prevailing background; colour combinations (e.g. black with an orange rim) are increasingly finding favour. Good-quality targets are essential in this discipline, with the 'g' force generated by the considerable launch speed likely to smash any inferior or damaged target. It goes without saying that at any competitive discipline, especially one aspiring to international status, the number of irregular targets caused by breakages off the trap arm must be kept to a minimum; this has encouraged the use of ultra-hard clays, and even though these do significantly reduce the number of breakages at launch, there may often be problems with targets not breaking when hit by the shot charge. This is naturally unacceptable to the shooters, many of whom struggle enough as it is to acquire a worthwhile score, and the target manufacturers are therefore engaged in perpetual pursuit of the ideal target which will withstand the high 'g' of target launch on the international Trap discipline yet break reasonably easily when hit by pellets.

Other equipment is basically as described in the last chapter dealing with DTL. Ammunition must be loaded with no more than 28 grammes of lead shot (1 ounce), while pellet size should not exceed 2.5 mm in diameter (number 6 shot English); favoured loads will contain either 7½s or 8s for the first shot, and because of the extra distances frequently involved due to the extreme speed of the target, many shooters use 7½s exclusively. Nickel loads are also highly rated, especially for second-barrel shots at targets which may be on the extreme limits of shotgun range, and where harder targets are to be encountered nickel loads are considered by some shooters to be an absolute necessity. Schools of thought do vary, however. Nickel shot can pass right through a target without achieving a break, while lead tends to flatten out on impact and thereby do more damage; conversely, the extra hitting power of nickel at long ranges cannot be denied, lead perhaps being too weak to break a target speeding away once maximum range has been reached. As in most facets of clay shooting, it is a case of experimentation before the shooter decides what is right for him.

For guns we need look no further than a standard Trap-shooting weapon as found on the DTL layout, although some shooters do use a slightly flatter-shooting gun. In general, though, many shooters of the international Trap disciplines tend to favour tighter chokes for their ability to deliver better patterns over a great distance. The quick and efficient ABT shooter will be on to his target before it has gone perhaps 30 metres, for which a ½ choke barrel and number 8 shot will be quite adequate – indeed, any other combination may find the shooter over-gunned. However, such shooters are mostly found only at the top levels of the sport, and for the lesser mortal a tighter ¾ choke and 7½s is perhaps the better choice. The second barrel is almost without exception full choke, necessarily so because the target approaches and exceeds the maximum killing range of a 12-bore. The Trap shooter's accessories hold good from one discipline to another (see previous chapter).

With all the international Trap disciplines the instant release of the target is absolutely critical, with Rule 9.10 (b) allowing a 'No Bird' to be declared 'if the target is not thrown immediately after his [the shooter's] call'. To this end electrically controlled acoustic release systems are widely used and in general can be considered quicker, more consistent and therefore superior to manual release. Strictly speaking this is not allowed for in the rules, but it would be unthinkable for any major ABT shoot of international or championship status to be run without the availability of acoustic-release systems.

TECHNIQUE

While DTL shooting is all about rigid concentration on the line, with ABT the situation is slightly different because the composition and operation of the squad are somewhat different. Although there are five stands placed in an arc to the rear of the trap house, there are six shooters in each squad, the procedure being as follows. At the start of each round of twenty-five targets shooters one to five take up their allocated place on the available shooting stations, the sixth shooter standing behind and out of sight of the shooter occupying station 1. The shooter occupying station 1 calls for and fires at his first target; the shooter on station 2 does the same, and this procedure continues along the line. When the shooter on station 2 has finished firing, *and not before*, the shooter on station 1 moves to his right ready to take up his new position on station 2; at the same time the sixth shooter moves forward to occupy the now vacant station 1. This movement of shooters continues in a smooth ripple, with the shooter occupying station 5 moving behind the line to take up his position on station 1 as soon as it becomes vacant. This continues until all six shooters have shot their full allocation of twenty-five targets. Concentration therefore needs to be total as the shooters move steadily round the layout. The range of targets – delivered, remember, at random – is uncompromisingly varied, while target angles and variations are exaggerated by the constantly changing perspective encountered by the shooter as he moves from station to station.

The difficulty of ABT targets is clearly recognised by the fact that two shots are allowed at each target, with no loss of points for a second-barrel kill, as applies in DTL. Any second-barrel kill at ABT fully deserves maximum points due to the inherent problems encountered as the target streaks away. At this point it is worth expanding on the point raised briefly above that exponents of the two Trench disciplines do not necessarily favour ABT despite the initial superficial similarities. Many contend that the random distribution of targets is unfair – the same charge frequently being levelled at DTL. In theory an even spread of targets should be encountered, each shooter taking his chance when calling for the target. However, in practice this is not always so. A fortunate shooter will sometimes receive a high proportion of easier targets – straighter and more shallowly angled, perhaps – while it is just as likely that another shooter will receive a high proportion of harder-angled targets. Although the circumstances are the same for all competitors, not all receive the same share of hard and less hard targets. In this respect ABT *is* unfair when compared with the Trench disciplines, a point which will be discussed further in the following two chapters.

Stance and gun-hold position are as always of crucial importance. Notably, the majority of international Trap shooters adopt a fairly narrow stance although it may be slightly more open to the trap house than that seen on the DTL layout. This is basically in response to the wider spread of targets, so that the shooter who stands slightly more chest-on to the trap house can usually move more easily in response to the violently swinging angles than if he adopted the side-on stance of the DTL shooter. As with all things, it is very much a question of

experimentation followed by individual preference, but the majority of ABT shooters seem to opt for that more open stance and, indeed, this is a common trait among many of those who shoot the international Trap disciplines. Gun-hold position also varies greatly within a squad, a great deal depending on the speed of reaction of the individual shooter. Just as with DTL, it pays to vary gun-hold position in response to which station the shooter is currently occupying: station 1 encourages a hold position to the left of the left-hand corner of the trap house in anticipation of the violent left-handed target; station 2 calls for the gun-hold position to come in further towards the centre as the perceived angles are reduced; station 3 requires a near-central gun-hold position; while stations 4 and 5 see the gun-hold position pushed progressively out to the right in response to that right-handed angle. The height of the gun-hold position is undoubtedly the crucial factor, and affects how rapidly the shooter can get on to the target. The low hold position, whereby the shooter points his muzzles at or slightly

Mervyn Funnell using a high hold position for ABT

below the front lip of the trap house, allows full and instant sight of the target almost as soon as it emerges and limits the likelihood of those lowest targets getting away; on the debit side, the inevitably rapid swinging up of the muzzles necessary when chasing a climbing target may result in a miss above. The higher hold position, whereby the shooter may hold his muzzles anything up to 3 or 4 feet above the trap house, can also have its drawbacks, there being a distinct danger of the lower targets getting away quickly before they are seen; on the plus side, the less extreme targets can be picked out and broken very quickly and with a significant degree of ease. Once again it is horses for courses, and for the newcomer ABT will doubtless occupy both mind and body for many years before a clear way forward is discovered.

When it comes actually to shooting ABT many of the comments relating to DTL apply, although the more violent angles and greater speeds will inevitably have an effect on target address. Those who consciously see lead – or who believe they see lead – will soon be aware that any attempt to measure lead, as in DTL, on those angled targets will quickly result in failure; shooting ABT is very much an instinctive thing, the speed of swing ensuring that the requisite lead has been taken up. Any shooter switching from DTL to ABT is bound to experience initial difficulties in dealing with the extra speed, something which only practice can put right; conversely, the shooter who changes back again to DTL often experiences all manner of problems because of the slowness of the targets.

HIGH STANDARDS

As an international discipline ABT does not have the domestic A/A class, although there are still four main classes – A, B, C and D. It is a fairly testing sport, the qualifying percentage for inclusion in A class being set at 90 per cent. Generally ABT is not as widely available (nor as popular) as DTL. There are, however, shooting grounds which specialise in this discipline, and so ABT availability is likely to be on a localised basis. A glance at the Members' Averages book for 1989/90 confirms this situation, with not much more than a dozen shooters returning over 2000 Registered targets and only about fifty returning over 1000; of these, Lady shooter P. Parsons shot the most with 2850 targets for a D class average of 75.6 per cent. Highest average was recorded by top Olympic Trap shooter Ian Peel with 96.4 per cent, although this was achieved over only 250 targets. I suspect that the main advocates of ABT are pleased that he sticks to other disciplines for the most part!

14 Olympic Trap

Known variously as Olympic Trench or 15-Trap, this is *the* discipline to most Trap shooters. As the names suggests, this is the form of Trap competed for at the Olympic Games, in which fifteen traps are set to offer targets to the competitor. Competition for international honours is fierce, with high stakes and fantastic rewards for the successful. Olympic Gold is undoubtedly the supreme accolade for any sportsman – whether he be shooter or sprinter – and there can be few greater incentives in the shooting world. It is a supremely challenging sport, although there are those who contend that the essentially similar Universal Trench is in fact the more testing discipline. Whether or not this is so does not alter the fact that Olympic Trap (OT) is the glamour discipline in the clay-shooting world, and there is a certain special atmosphere surrounding any big competition at which all the top shooters are present.

THE LAYOUT

Olympic trap requires a full-blown international Trap layout; it is one which is versatile enough to accommodate ABT and Universal Trench, but is in essence designed to provide special targets for specialist shooters. As the line drawing demonstrates, the OT layout is a radical departure from the curved arc of shooting stations found in both DTL and ABT. Again there are five shooting stations, but this time they are set 49 feet 2 inches (15 m) behind the front lip of a trench designed to hold the banks of traps. The specifications and settings of an OT layout are at first glance complex, but with the aid of the line drawing are essential reading if the shooter is to understand how the discipline works and therefore not to become totally overawed by it. Basically the OT layout is set up as follows. The roof of the trench is level with the shooting stations, and also ideally level with the ground, and the trench is a minimum of 9 feet 9 inches (3 m) deep from front to rear. The positioning of the traps is vitally important: each shooting station has in front of it three traps, clays delivered to that station coming from these three traps *only*, and there are five banks of traps corresponding with the positioning of the shooting stations; the centre

OT shooter moves
on to a higher
target, Garlands
Sporting Ground

of station 1 corresponds with the centre of the second trap in the first bank of three, which in turn is between 6 feet 6 inches and 9 feet 9 inches (2–3 m) in from the left-hand wall of the trench itself; thereafter each of the other two traps is 3 feet 3 inches to 3 feet 7 inches (1.0–1.1 m) at centre either side of that central trap. Centres are very important in setting up Trap layouts, and although there may well be a fair degree of tolerance on layouts from one to another, the centres must remain constant one to another. Thus from the centre of station 1 to the centre of station 2 the traps must be between 9 feet 9 inches and 19 feet 8 inches (3–6 m), and thereafter in the same proportion until five shooting stations have been set.

Each trap in turn is preset to throw a certain target, so that the inherent unfairnesses built into the DTL and ABT forms of Trap shooting cannot blight the OT shooter. In OT everyone has exactly the same proportion of targets, although not all in the same order; thus if your particular bogey target is the sharp, low left-hander, at least you can feel safe in the knowledge that you are not going to receive an inordinate number of these. During the round of twenty-five targets the shooter knows that he will receive a total of ten left-handers, ten right-handers and five straight, shared equally among the five banks of traps, and it is possible to calculate with a degree of precision just

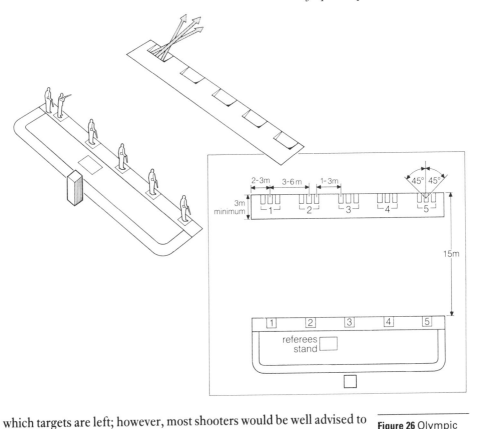

Figure 26 Olympic Trap layout

which targets are left; however, most shooters would be well advised to forget about such off-putting distractions and concentrate on smashing each target as it comes. Each trap is set to throw its target at a different speed, which poses many problems for the shooter in that he cannot become thoroughly accustomed to the speed of target (as he can with ABT for example). This factor calls for a high degree of sophistication in the OT layout, with acoustic-release and computerised control systems absolutely vital. In order to retain continuity the computer operator must be able to reset the system after a broken or otherwise irregular target; where this occurs the shooter will, of course, know with absolute certainty what type of target he is going to receive.

The carrying distance of the target varies according to the set height, although at its optimum height of 6 feet 6 inches (2 m) above level ground at 32 feet 6 inches (10 m) from the trap, it will travel 262 feet (80 m). This makes it by far the fastest of all Trap targets, and adds up to a very formidable challenge indeed. The maximum angle is set at 45 degrees either side of centre. There are a number of published OT Setting Tables, and competitions should conform to one of them. Number 1, which is reproduced here, shows how varied the flight of OT targets are in terms of height, angle and distance. Although the tables may vary significantly one from another they must nevertheless all conform to certain criteria; the targets must fly no lower than 4 feet 9 inches (1.50 m) above level ground at 32 feet 6 inches (10 m) from the trap, and no higher than 11 feet 1 inch (3.50 m); similarly they must travel no less than 230 feet (70 m) and no further than 262 feet (80 m).

EQUIPMENT

The traps are usually small electric-release versions, often with a short arm to enable the target to reach maximum speed very quickly. This can create the same problem of broken clays mentioned in the last chapter, and so again clays are needed which are hard enough to withstand the 'g' force created in launch, while being sufficiently fragile to break when struck by the shot charge. Many of the top grounds use purpose-built OT traps, such as the Laporte, and combine these with hard Laporte clays. It is one of the perennial problems facing OT shooters, who often tackle it by using high-power loads of nickel shot. But no matter which shot is used, it must be within the 28 gramme (1 ounce) limit of the maximum 2.5 mm (number 6 English) shot, although with increasingly sophisticated manufacturing techniques this creates few problems these days.

Once again the gun leans towards the heavy, tightly choked Trap version, although for OT fewer shooters risk the sort of relatively open borings which the ABT enthusiast can make do with; the option of tight chokes – frequently ¾ and full or even full and full – is usually preferred although some of the better Shots can undoubtedly achieve good results with a ½ choke first barrel. In general, however, the use of tight chokes is widespread, justifiably so as the shooter is confronted with those fast hard targets. Few OT shooters seem to favour the sort of high-shooting Trap gun so commonly found on the DTL range, a much flatter-shooting gun being more suited to this discipline. This has evolved in response to the flat fast OT target (indeed, this can be seen across the whole spectrum of international Trap) which a high-shooting gun might struggle to get below. I have been told by more than one OT shooter that he likes his gun to shoot where he is looking. Be that as it may, a wide variety of Trap gun types are to be seen on the OT range, and individual preference, as always, varies significantly; however, even if the high-shooting gun might prove an asset against the higher targets, it must be a liability when confronted with a target flying at the lower end of the spectrum.

TECHNIQUE

As with ABT, there is a six-man squad, with the shooters moving after each and every shot. Many of the premises outlined in ABT hold good for OT; most certainly the narrow, yet slightly open stance will prove a necessity in dealing with fast targets, many of which will be sharply angled into the bargin. This stance is very much a question of compromise: if the stance is too open the shooter will find his swing inhibited, particularly on the targets which fly back across the body (the right-hander for the right-handed shooter); if the stance is too narrow instability will increase and the sharply angled targets will again cause a serious problem. It is very much a question of practising until the ideal format is arrived at. The gun-hold position offers a similar dilemma, the choice of high or low position being a question of individual preference. However, the very fast OT targets do not allow quite the same degree of latitude as in ABT, and the shooter who adopts the low gun-hold position on or around the target exit point will need to be blessed with very quick reactions. The majority of OT shooters opt for a moderately high gun-hold position – perhaps 3 feet above the target exit point – and this allows them to get after the target with the minimum of delay while at the same time lessening the risk of a jerky movement, which will only result in missed targets. Hard as it may seem when confronted with the fastest targets in the clay-shooting world, the shooter must strive for a smooth, controlled swing.

Any perception of lead when shooting OT is almost certainly an illusion, and any shooter who attempts to calculate lead will be wasting his time. Even more than with ABT, shooting must be instinctive if it is to succeed; yes, the angled targets do need plenty of lead in order to achieve a hit, but the shooter really must rely on instinctive swing and follow-through simply because the targets are travelling so very fast. This instinctive reaction must be adopted throughout each round of OT, for the lesser angles and straight targets are seldom very much slower even if they appear to be so; the shooter will have no time to mess about with high-shooting guns or any other aid to success – it is him against the target, with no frills or fuss.

HIGH STANDARDS

As with all the international disciplines, the relative dearth of facilities has an effect on the numbers of shooters coming through to the highest levels. This is especially true of the Trench disciplines, which are so expensive to install and maintain; it is certainly true of OT with its fifteen traps and ancillaries, and it is rare indeed for a new shooting ground to offer a Trench layout. Where OT is on offer the response for the major shoots is excellent, the limiting factor sometimes being the length of the day rather than the number of potential entrants.

Britain has been blessed with some very good OT shooters over the years. Many clay shooters fondly remember the heroics of Bob Braithwaite as he won Olympic Gold – the only Briton thus far to achieve this feat in clay shooting. More recently Kevin Gill and Ian Peel returned home from the Commonwealth Games with medals, and as I write these two men can give anyone in the world a good run for their money. So the state of the discipline seems good, although this is perhaps more by virtue of the excellence of a few individuals rather than any wider buoyancy. The qualifying percentages for the classes reflect the difficulty of the discipline, which has the lowest qualifying percentage per class of any Trap discipline – 87 per cent or above being required to achieve A class rating. Despite the comparative lack of facilities a select band of shooters pursue OT with single-minded determination, and some twenty-two shooters recorded over 2000 Registered targets in 1989/90. Only one returned over 3000 targets: A. Cliffe, with 3300, for a class A average of 88.6 per cent, an excellent display of consistent shooting. Top average is attributed to Peter Croft with an astonishing 95.2 per cent achieved over 1000 targets.

The main difference with OT is the sequence settings affecting how the discipline will be shot. With OT there are nine of these Setting Tables, controlling angle, elevation and speed (distance). No. 5 is reproduced by way of example.

Group	Number of traps	Direction of trajectory from the trap	Elevation of trajectory at 10m level ground	Length of trajectory
1	n.1	45° to right	1m 60	75m
	n.2	0°	3m	75m
	n.3	45° to left	2m	70m
2	n.4	40° to right	2m 80	80m
	n.5	10° to left	1m 50	70m
	n.6	45° to left	2m	78m
3	n.7	35° to right	3m	70m
	n.8	5° to left	1m 80	80m
	n.9	40° to left	1m 50	72m
4	n.10	25° to right	1m 80	75m
	n.11	0°	1m 60	70m
	n.12	30° to left	3m 40	72m
5	n.13	30° to right	2m	75m
	n.14	10° to right	2m 40	72m
	n.15	15° to left	1m 80	70m

15 *Universal Trench*

Universal Trench (UT) is very similar in many ways to Olympic Trap, with the same layout sufficing for both disciplines although there are some notable differences. Once again the shooter is confronted with a super-fast Trap target. However, there the similarities end and we need to look at UT in a whole new light to understand what it is that makes this version of Trap so distinct. It is widely known among shooters as '5-Trap' a term which accurately and succinctly sums it up. In the opinion of many of its devotees UT is the most difficult of all the Trap disciplines, surpassing even OT, and there may well be some substance in this assertion. However, there is no need to make such direct comparisons; it is sufficient to recognise that it is a very demanding discipline indeed.

THE LAYOUT

The layout described for OT doubles nicely for UT, shooting-station dimensions, trap-house dimensions and distance from stations to front of trench all being broadly the same, as the line drawing bears out. It is in the trench itself that the most significant differences occur, there being five traps instead of the fifteen found in OT. Once again centres are crucial, the centre of number 3 shooting station aligning with the centre of the third trap; thereafter trap centres are 3 feet 3 inches to 3 feet 9 inches (1.00–1.25 m) apart to the left and the right of that centre trap until all five traps are located in line. The full spread of five traps can be accommodated within a frontage of 19 feet 8 inches (6 m), while the full spread of five shooting stations occupies a line of 36 feet (11 m). The shooter is therefore confronted with a central bank of five traps significantly narrower than the spread of traps encountered in OT, and any one of them may release on demand. As with OT the height of targets over level ground is set at 32 feet 6 inches (10 m) in front of that centre trap, and the minimum height is 5 feet (1.5 m) with a maximum of 11 feet 6 inches (3.5 m). Ten Universal Trench schemes exist which deliver a variety of targets with varying angles, heights and speeds; the maximum angles are 45 degrees either side of centre on each trap, while the maximum carrying distance is 230 feet

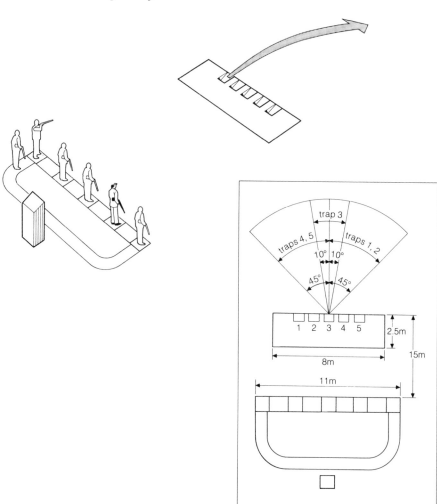

Figure 27 Universal Trench layout

(70 m) with a minimum distance of 197 feet (60 m). The sample scheme reproduced here is Scheme 5. As may be seen, there can be substantial variation in target angles and heights, while a 32 foot 6 inch (10 m) variation in target carrying distance can amount to a considerable difference in terms of speed.

EQUIPMENT

The traps and ancillaries are, of course, the key to the layout. As with OT, single short-arm dedicated traps are used to ensure maximum target speed immediately after launch, and therefore the comments relating to OT and ABT concerning fragility of targets at launch and hardness of targets in relation to cartridge killing ability apply equally to this discipline. Older layouts may use converted single-arm traps of

many types, but today the sort of specialist trap described in the chapter dealing with OT is widely used. Otherwise what serves well for OT will be ideal for UT, including guns and cartridges.

UT shooting at
Thurlaston Gun
Club

TECHNIQUE

Technique similar to that used in OT will also serve the UT shooter well, with one major exception. Instead of facing a dedicated bank of traps directly in front of his position, the shooter can expect a target from any one of the five traps; this gives the shooter some very sharp angles, and even though the angles *at the trap* are no more severe than those encountered in OT, the fact that the shooter's position relative to the trap changes so radically throughout a round of twenty-five can mean that violently swinging angles occur, the like of which are not encountered in any other discipline. So for the shooter standing on shooting station number 1, a sharp left-handed target from trap 5 (that is, at the far right-hand end of the layout) will race across him at an astonishing speed, which will create a problem out of all proportion to its 45-degree angle of flight. The same sort of problem will confront the shooter standing on shooting station number 5 and receiving a sharp right-hander from trap 1. A whole range of targets in between these extremes will be encountered, making UT an enormous challenge. Yet as with OT, UT is scrupulously fair, delivering the same targets to each shooter, although again not necessarily in the

UT squad in action

same order. Once again this is achieved via the computer and the scheme chosen for the day. As with OT, the gun-hold position is very much a matter of personal preference and will be arrived at as a result of experience. The great majority of experienced shooters adopt a high position, and with a discipline comprising so many difficult targets it is vitally important that the target is given no opportunity to dash away before the shooter has time to react. Lateral gun-hold position should vary as with other Trap disciplines, and will alter according to which shooting station is currently being occupied; in this way the shooter will be best equipped to face the challenge ahead, although even then only the sharpest of performers are likely to return better than average scores.

As with the other international Trap disciplines, both barrels may be used on a target, and the result of such shots count equally – quite rightly, too, as any shooter who manages to break this type of fast target with a second shot deserves all the credit they can get. Trap shooters undoubtedly develop the art of accurate second-barrel shooting to an extraordinary degree, as they must do if they are to succeed on a consistent basis. With a rising target – as all Trap targets are – the first shot invariably takes that target at its optimum point, so that thereafter it begins to level out or even drop, which inevitably poses all sorts of problems. Second-barrel shooting is all about experience in Trap shooting; from that experience comes the split-second timing needed to break targets with a second shot. This is a vital part of the Trap shooter's art.

HIGH STANDARDS

If anything UT facilities are even more sparsely spread throughout the country than are those for OT, with a following of correspondingly smaller proportions. The qualifying averages once again testify to the extreme difficulty of the discipline, 88 per cent and above being necessary to achieve a class A rating. The relative lack of facilities is graphically illustrated by the fact that very few shooters returned over 1000 Registered targets in the year 1989/90. Top return is accredited to A. Wright with 1875 targets for a class A average of 88.9 per cent, while the top average of 96 per cent is the joint distinction of M. Jones and A. Wells – even though both of them shot no more than the bare minimum of a hundred targets, which creates a false picture. A clearer impression of the actual standards set by those who shoot UT regularly is easier to attain by analysing the averages of those who did shoot over 1000 Registered targets; this shows that very few shooters indeed broke over 90 per cent, R. Fletton coming top with 92.8 per cent over his 1700 targets – a remarkable performance by any standards.

With Universal Trench there are ten schemes designed to set angle elevation and speed (distance). Reproduced here is Scheme 5.

| | | *Angle* | | *Height* | |
Scheme	*Trap No.*	*Left*	*Right*	*(at 10m)*	*Distance*
	1		45°	2.5m	65m
	2		30°	3.0m	60m
5	3		5°	2.0m	60m
	4	30°		3.5m	70m
	5	40°		2.0m	65m

16 Double-Trap and ZZ

Double-trap and ZZ are on the edge of the clay-shooting scene in terms of availability and participation. Despite the fact that both are international disciplines, with Great Britain team places available for successful shooters, interest seems to remain low. Various reasons for this undoubtedly exist, the recent introduction of Double-trap probably accounting for its current small following, while with ZZ the high cost of both practice and competitive shooting must surely be a limiting factor. Nevertheless, to complete any analysis of clay shooting in Britain today we must take a look at both, even if only superficially.

DOUBLE-TRAP

This is the newest of all the clay-pigeon disciplines, and is in reality a created discipline for international competition designed specifically with the media (television in particular) in mind. Accusations that the present Olympic disciplines of Trap and ISU Skeet were not exciting enough to encourage widespread spectator interest eventually led to a near-blackmail situation where the implication was that unless clay shooting was spruced up it might be dropped from the Olympics altogether. Because Olympic participation is still the clay shooter's highest accolade, it was obvious that the threat to participation needed to be taken seriously, so the UIT was directed to introduce a new form of clay shooting. Earliest attempts led to the introduction of a basically unfair discipline which utilised two traps, one of which oscillated and threw its target at random. This meant that with good fortune, an individual shooter could receive a disproportionate number of easier targets, and so the dislike by 'proper' Trap shooters for the *ad hoc* targets presented in ABT found a new focus in the embryonic Double-trap, with an inevitably unfavourable reaction among the very people who could make or break the discipline – the shooters themselves. It was perceived by them as being unfair and very difficult, with even the top participants struggling to turn in either good or consistent scores.

In revamping the discipline to make it fair enough to tempt shooters into competing, the UIT had to bear in mind the needs of television –

the object of the initial exercise. The targets therefore needed to be reasonably high, with such height fairly uniform between the two targets. The scrapping of the oscillating trap dealt with the fairness aspect, while the introduction of an OT or UT type scheme of target distribution fulfilled many of the aspirations of established Trap shooters. Suddenly Double-trap was a worthy discipline, and thanks to guaranteed international status and the inherent rewards affecting such a discipline, it was one worth competing in. Three traps were introduced in place of the original two, making it possible to use an OT layout utilising the three centre traps. As with other Trap disciplines, the shooter operates around a layout of five shooting stations; in the case of Double-trap the shooter receives five pairs of targets from each station, making twenty-five pairs in all (a fifty-target course). The traps are preset according to the scheme in use but must conform to the following criteria: the left-hand trap is set at between o degrees (straight) and 15 degrees to the left; the centre trap is set anywhere between 5 degrees either side of centre; the right-hand trap is set between o degrees and 15 degrees to the right. Each shooter receives two pairs from traps 1 and 2; two pairs from traps 2 and 3; and one pair from traps 1 and 3, although as with the other international Trap disciplines of OT and UT, the sequences vary. However, by the end of the layout each shooter will have received precisely the same targets as all others in a squad, and in this way Double-trap can be considered fair to everyone. The traps are set to throw targets between 181 feet (55 m) and 260 feet 6 inches (65 m), making Double-trap slightly slower than the other international Trap disciplines. However, the fact that both targets are released simultaneously means that it is quite challenging enough already, without the addition of ultra-fast targets as well. Height is set at between 9 feet 9 inches (3 m) and 11 feet 6 inches (3.5 m), this extra height taking account of the demands of television.

Most Double-trap shooters tend to use the sort of gun suitable for use in OT and UT. The comments on dealing with the domestic discipline of Double-rise will probably stand the shooter in good stead here, although the variations in angle, height and speed make Double-trap altogether more demanding; but the general precept of trying to establish a calm and unhurried approach to the pairs, in an attempt to find a neat rhythmic pattern, does apply, and the shooter will be well advised to pursue this line of approach. Gun-hold position should take account of the fact that all the targets consistently fly higher than in other international disciplines, and the accent must be on a quick first-barrel kill without losing that all-important rhythm. Cartridge loads are as for other Trap disciplines, and because that second target is always a long way out it is well worth investing in a top-class second-barrel load – possibly with nickel-coated pellets.

ZZ

As discussed in the earliest chapters of this book, ZZ (zig-zag) shooting evolved in direct response to the needs of those whose first love was the shooting of live birds. With live-bird shooting (usually pigeons but also starlings and other birds) outlawed in many countries, the need arose to develop a realistic alternative, particularly as the so-called 'clay pigeon' scarcely fitted the bill. The artificial pigeon ZZ target was devised to fill the void. The set-up of the sport is virtually identical to that found in live-pigeon shooting, and the total unpredictability of the flying ZZ target bears a great resemblance to the desperate escape flight of a released bird.

The target itself is released from a launcher which rotates it at speeds of several thousand revolutions per minute, so that when it takes off, the spinning winged target can perform some really crazy manoeuvres. Targets consist of two orange wings and a central body, into which is pressed a white disc: its configuration means that the target's flight is completely unpredictable, and it can fly right or left at any elevation while being apt to zig-zag in flight (the manoeuvre from which the name derives). The object of the exercise, as it is with live-bird shooting, is not simply to kill the target but to kill it so that it lands within a perimeter fence, and therefore it is part of the art of ZZ shooting to break the target quickly and effectively. Many a championship has been won and lost by the broken target falling fractionally out of bounds. Hence the widespread use of heavy loads, 1 1/4 oz being the accepted ZZ load; anyone using anything less was considered undergunned. Despite the new light-load revolution sweeping clay shooting, maximum loads remain unchanged; size stipulations also remain unaltered, anything between number 6 and 9 English being permissible. The object is to knock the white centre from the speeding target, and for that centre to fall within the perimeter.

The ZZ specifications are as follows. The layout is designed around a flat area of land some 165 feet (50 m) in diameter surrounded by a 2-foot (0.6 m) high fence. The five launching traps are positioned in the centre of this ring, and are spaced 16 feet 6 inches (5 m) apart; the shooter operates as an individual rather than in a squad as most Trap shooters tend to do, and he is positioned 82 feet 6 inches (25 m) behind the line of traps. On the command 'Pull' one of the traps opens and releases a ZZ target, and it is then up to the shooter to react as quickly and as accurately as possible, with either barrel available with which to record a kill; under certain circumstances, particularly if the target is assisted by any available wind, the shooter will do very well indeed to be successful with his second barrel. The targets are apt to be wayward in the extreme, and may fly high or low. To take this into account many ZZ shooters use a fairly flat-shooting gun – one which shoots more to the point of aim. For instance, Linda Savage (1990 European Ladies' Champion) uses a Beretta SO3 and her choice is not an uncommon one, the Beretta SO range being widely used.

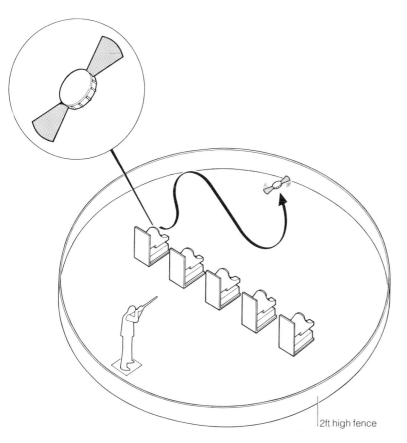

Figure 28 ZZ target and layout

2ft high fence

17 *National and International Honours*

The ardent competitor probably sees a team place as the ultimate achievement. Whether that place is in the national or Great Britain team, the struggle is every bit as fierce. It is a great honour to be included in the Great Britain team for the international disciplines, in which the successful shooter may even achieve the glory of a medal at Commonwealth or Olympic Games level. Unlike many sports' selection procedures, clay-shooting team places are decided strictly on merit; there is none of the favouritism and bias often alleged to occur in sports where selectors are used, such as football or cricket. In clay shooting the best scores qualify the shooter for a place – end of story. Each shooter therefore knows where he stands right from the outset, and there can be no inexplicable exclusion of individuals currently in top form. Not that this makes it any easier to gain a team place – remarkably consistent form is required to see the shooter through.

The criteria for 1990 team selection are an indication of the sort of dedication needed to qualify. With the home internationals for English Skeet and Down-the-Line it is still mostly a case of shooting as much as possible, which to a degree may limit qualifiers to those with the deepest pockets. In the case of the teams for English Sporting and the international disciplines (both national and Great Britain teams) there are set selection shoots from which the best scores are taken. For Great Britain teams a continuous points accumulation procedure is used, the competitor with the fewest number of points standing highest in the rankings.

ENGLAND DOWN-THE-LINE TEAM

This is by far the largest of the England teams competing in the home internationals, and comprises thirty Seniors, five Ladies and five Juniors. For Seniors the scores to be taken into account are the best *six* scores made at any hundred-bird CPSA-Registered DTL Selection Shoot, of which there are eleven in number. For Ladies and Juniors the best *four* scores achieved at any of the above-mentioned Selection Shoots will count.

Throughout the Selection Shoot series, the 'points' system will

operate; those returning the lowest points total will comprise the England team. Following on from the Selection Shoots will be a compulsory 200-bird event, with the 'points' system once again applying.

Final squad for an ISU Skeet Selection Shoot

ENGLAND SKEET TEAM

The team consists of ten Seniors, two Ladies and two Juniors. For Seniors the best *six* hundred-bird scores made at CPSA-Registered events held between 1 June and 15 April *plus* the score achieved at the English Skeet Championship apply. For Ladies and Juniors the best *three* hundred-bird scores, from three different grounds, *plus* the score attained at the English Skeet Championship is the rule. The Senior team consists of the nine shooters with the best aggregates, *plus* the highest-scoring shooter from the English Skeet Championship. No more than two scores can be submitted from any one ground.

ENGLISH SPORTING TEAM

The team consists of fifteen Seniors, two Ladies and two Juniors. There are five designated Selection Shoots, one in each CPSA region, plus the British Open Sporting Championship and the English Open Sporting Championship; applicants must submit their best *four* scores. The points system is used to select team members.

153

A slightly different format applies for the international disciplines. As with English Sporting, team places are decided by a points system, with the results obtained from Selection Shoots counting. However, all the Selection Shoots are two-day affairs, consisting of two hundred targets plus a mandatory extra twenty-five targets for the six top-scoring shooters over the two days. This is a real test of consistent shooting and it is the better shooters who generally come out on top.

ENGLISH ISU SKEET TEAM

The Team comprises twelve members. The points system of selection is used, with the best *three* scores from the four ISU Skeet Selection Shoots counting.

ENGLAND OLYMPIC TRAP TEAM

The team comprises twelve members. The points system of selection is used, with the best *two* scores from the three OT Selection Shoots counting.

ENGLAND AUTOMATIC BALL TRAP TEAM

The team comprises twelve members. The points system of selection is used, with the *three* best scores from the four ABT Selection Shoots counting.

Those who qualify for the major internationals as members of the Great Britain team can expect to shoot over at least three days, with seventy-five targets on each of the first two days and a further fifty on the final day. It is a demanding schedule requiring the utmost concentration over a prolonged period – something which most shooters in this country are not used to. It is therefore fairly surprising that Great Britain shooters perform as well as they do when travelling abroad.

For ISU Skeet and Olympic Trap the teams are decided on the points system over the best three scores obtained from the last four Selection Shoots. Each year a punishing list of competitions awaits the candidates: for 1990 the list included the World Championship (Moscow); European Championship (Sweden); European Grand Prix (Austria); Nations Grand Prix (Italy); and World Cups in Italy, East Germany and Holland.

A similar set-up exists for both the FITASC disciplines of FITASC Sporting and Universal Trench. The CPSA's British International Board continuous assessment system is used, with three out of four Selection Shoot scores to count. For FITASC Sporting there are the

Ken Harman

World Championship (France); European Championship (Cyprus); and FITASC Grand Prix (Great Britain). For UT there is the World Championship (Italy) and European Championship (Portugal).

So it can be seen that the successful international shooter needs to have talent aplenty; he will also need to be determined, resourceful and able to foot the not inconsiderable bill for his expensive hobby. It is a tall order, but one which British shooters have proved themselves well up to. The 1990 Commonwealth Games is a case in point: in the Olympic Trap Pairs event England won gold (K. Gill and I. Peel), with Wales winning silver (J. Birkett-Evans and C. Evans); in the individual England won silver (K. Gill) and bronze (I. Peel). The success story continued in the ISU Skeet Pairs, Scotland winning gold (J. Dunlop and I. Marsden), and England taking silver (K. Harman and A. Austin); in the individual, England won the gold (K. Harman) and bronze (A. Austin). All in all, it was a remarkable performance by Britain's top clay shooters. In addition, there was the success of John Grice at Universal Trench, in which he won the gold in the World Championship and the bronze in the European Championship. Obviously team honours are not easily attained, but nevertheless the achievements of these top shooters set a marvellous example to up-and-coming competitors.

18 The Champion

It is very difficult for the ordinary clay shooter to understand how the champion really ticks. What motivates him? How does his mind work? What preparations are necessary before a successful assault on some major title? During the preparation of this book I spoke to a few of these men and women, all outstanding Shots in their own discipline. All are very different people with differing mentalities, each pursuing a different facet of a complex sport; yet they are bound together by a common factor – all are winners at the highest level, ordinary clay-shooting fanatics who have worked hard to reach the top. Almost without exception they are nice people, although obviously intensely different: Andy Austin, the brilliant ISU Skeet specialist, seems a quiet introvert; George Digweed – one of the finest Sporting Shots of modern times – a bubbling extrovert. The names included in this chapter are some of the very best contemporary Shots. From each of them we could all learn something to help us enhance our own shooting ability.

JOHN GRICE – 1990 UNIVERSAL TRENCH WORLD CHAMPION

Of all clay-shooting disciplines Universal Trench is perhaps the least known; outside of the sport itself it is virtually unheard of, and even among the majority of clay-shooting regulars it is a largely unfamiliar and uncared-for discipline. Yet to participants it is Trap shooting *par excellence*, claimed by some to be even more demanding than the better-known Olympic Trap. Most certainly it has never had a particularly high profile, and has been perhaps the least glamorous of the big Trap events.

All that changed in dramatic fashion during 1990, when a Staffordshire man named John Grice took the Trench world by storm to defeat the Italian experts on their own ground. The scene: Lonato, Italy. The event: the 1990 Universal Trap World Championship, with 359 competitors. The score: 195 ex 200. For John Grice it was to be the pinnacle of a successful Trap-shooting career, even though he is no stranger to the victory rostrum, having won both British and

English titles twice over. As the man himself says, 'Once you have won the World Championship there is nowhere else to go – you've done it all.'

John Grice

Later in the same year he took on the Italians again, this time in the European Championships in Vilamora, Portugal. Once again he shot a 195, but this time the Italians came ready for him and he had to settle for third place and the bronze medal. Then came the disappointment of being forced to miss the World Cup tournament, a financially constrained British International Board being unable to find the money to send a team; with a nine-point lead accumulated from the World and European, John Grice was a virtual certainty to lift this title, too – sadly, it was not to be.

Unlike participants in some of the other more widely available disciplines, no Universal Trench shooter manages to clock up huge totals of Registered targets, and because of this, such winning achievements by any Briton are all the more remarkable. Practice is of

157

course vital to ultimate success, but John Grice takes a slightly more laid-back attitude to non-competitive targets than many of his rivals, being happy to shoot consistently at levels of around 22–23 ex 25. He says, 'I believe that you've only got so many twenty-fives in you, and I want to save them for the real thing!' No, he does not shoot below his best deliberately, just prefers not to subject himself to the pressure needed to succeed at the highest levels.

Pre-shoot preparation is almost totally a mental exercise. The target practice is important in that it keeps the body sharp and keen, but as all clay shooters are well aware, it is the mind that is all-important. 'You have to believe that you're the best, know that you're the best and that on the day you can beat anyone.' Throughout the shooting day John is just one of the boys, but as squadding time approaches he needs to get away from everyone else for a while as he runs the targets over and over in his mind, shooting each one mentally so that he really is hyped up by the time the first target dashes out from under the muzzles.

After the World Championship came huge publicity and acclaim, not just from the shooting press. At last the wider public was beginning to hear about Universal Trench, and from that John Grice can draw extra satisfaction. The reaction of other shooters towards him has been excellent, as they acknowledge the wonderful feat in beating the best in the world in a sport essentially dominated by non-British shooters. If there is a down-side to the whole affair it is that everyone now looks to John Grice as the winner of every competition he enters, although this, of course, takes no account of the many other fine Universal Trench shooters working the circuit in this country. He does not find this a problem, for when he is on the line it is 100 per cent concentration the whole time: 'I am aware of nothing else except that next target.' Anyone who watches John Grice shoot and witnesses the total concentration and lightning reactions to ultra-fast targets cannot doubt for a moment that there are more titles to come for this man.

ANDY AUSTIN – 1990 ENGLISH CHAMPION INTERNATIONAL SKEET

Skeet shooting is in many ways a total contrast to the world of Trap. Gone is the cloistered – some might say suffocating – atmosphere generated on the Trap line; in its stead is a somewhat more casual approach, although to minimise the intensity of the Skeet shooters' approach is to make a grave error. Basically Skeet shooters can walk about as they shoot their twenty-five; they have time to analyse their own performance without becoming overwrought; concentration seems to come in fits and starts, and even a squad competing at the highest level seems able to enjoy an exchange of words or to share a joke. Skeet shooters think their Trap counterparts are crazy. As one

SKEET

It's over – Andy Austin after breaking his last target for the English ISU title – Market Harborough Gun Club

top Shot told me when I said I shot Trap: 'Well, I suppose somebody has to!'

Yet watching Andy Austin going for his fourth English Grand Prix title was to watch a man momentarily apart from his fellows. His level of concentration seemed to be more intense, the pressure almost tangible as he neared the end of that marathon 225-target course; on the last day he seemed to be a man who felt assured of his destiny. Afterwards, as he waited for the rest of the squad to finish, it was almost possible to see the pressure wash out of him: 'It was hard work out there!'

The fact that International Skeet, in common with the Trench disciplines, is hard to come by makes the performances of such men as Andy Austin all the more remarkable. Practice is not achieved without a good deal of effort and expense, although the fact that he lives near Bedford and is ideally placed to travel to many shooting grounds in the centre of the country is an undoubted asset. None the less, the amount of competitive shooting available is strictly limited, which means that any achievements on the international scene are all the more impressive. One or two top shooters even have their own layouts, which makes the routine hundred or so targets a week, intensifying to a couple of hundred before a big shoot, more easily attainable. ISU is an intensely demanding discipline, requiring faultless technique and timing allied to the lightning reflexes necessary to deal with ultra-fast targets; it is very much a discipline requiring maximum commitment and dedication, no comparable targets being available elsewhere in the clay-pigeon world. Gun handling aside, there is no great benefit to be gained from other forms of practice – ISU really is in a class of its own.

Styles differ greatly in ISU and include a fair sprinkling of outlandish and seemingly uncomfortable ones, the crouch being high on the list of variations. All are doubtless viable, although Austin's classic erect stance is a fine model for up-and-coming shooters, and amazingly effective, too. It is a style which has taken him to the top in his sport on a regular basis, while his curiously laid-back approach towards big competition is refreshing to see. A good, genuine shooter whose approach to his sport is creditworthy, he has no flashy pretensions, just a quiet determination to succeed – a lesson for us all.

GEORGE DIGWEED – 1989 ENGLISH AND BRITISH CHAMPION ENGLISH SPORTING

English Sporting is among the most difficult of all clay-shooting disciplines, and is certainly the most demanding of all our domestic forms. As the qualifying average for the top A/A class proves, success on a consistent basis is hard to come by.

In 1989 George Digweed from Sussex created clay-shooting history by winning both the English Open Sporting and the British Open Sporting; by any standards it was a remarkable feat, and one which is unlikely to be repeated in a hurry. Always to be relied upon to turn in a good score, he has enjoyed a particularly successful run over the last year or two, even if 1990 was less kind to him in terms of prizes at English Sporting – he was unable to retain either title despite getting to a shoot-off situation for the British Open. However, four major FITASC Sporting titles more than made up for that. It is a measure of his all-round consistency that he enjoys top-class rating in several domestic disciplines: Sporting 91.2 per cent, DTL 96 per cent, Skeet 98 per cent; as well as a thoroughly creditable class A rating in the testing FITASC Sporting with 85 per cent. His 1990 successes included major FITASC championships, notably the Belgian and Dutch events.

George Digweed is one of the most outgoing shooters on the circuit. An extrovert of the highest order, he really has mastered his sport to an amazing degree, and this allied to the fact that he is still in his twenties must surely mean that he will be around as a top-notch clay shooter for a long time to come. Today he enjoys a significant level of sponsorship, which helps to provide the means for him to dominate the Sporting scene in the South-East. There are few decent-sized Open shoots in the region where his considerable presence is not to be found, and on his day there are few shooters capable of matching him.

Yet George has mellowed somewhat over the last year or two. Gone is the boastful cap displaying the logo 'Damn I'm Good!'. In its place is a quieter acceptance that he really is a good Shot and does not need to tell people about it. It may be a hackneyed saying that good shooting is no accident, but in his case it is particularly true. Even though George has always been good it took some self-analysis and a special resolve to achieve the outstanding feats of 1989. The accent was first on physical fitness, with more exercise based on the premise that a fit body leads to a fit mind; while on the mental side he accepted that it was not possible to remain sharp throughout the long summer competition season and concentrated instead on peaking at the critical times. Now he shoots all the time just as he did in the old days, the bonus being that there are plenty of English Sporting shoots in the South-East for him to practise on. But the winning is not quite so important until it comes to the major events. It is a scenario which works for George Digweed and is a fair mirror image of the kind of tactics used by other top shooters. The year 1990 may have seen new English and British champions in English Sporting, but I would not want to wager money against George Digweed coming back with a vengeance over the next year or two.

LINDA SAVAGE – 1990 EUROPEAN LADIES' ZZ CHAMPION

Britain has produced some excellent women clay shooters, and the Sporting Ladies have done particularly well over the last few years. If there is any discipline where they regularly overwhelm the opposition, it is undoubtedly ZZ. A relatively new discipline in Britain, with its power base in Kent, it is a great tribute to its devotees that they are able to take on the best from Europe and win with amazing regularity at what is essentially a very continental sport.

Linda Savage is well known among Trap shooters in south-east England, the Trap-shooting bias seemingly being an ideal training ground for the harsh demands made by competitive ZZ shooting. In 1990 she was part of the thirteen-strong Great Britain team which went to Paris to compete in the two-day European Championship, playing a magnificent part in the triumph enjoyed by Seniors, Ladies and Juniors – with only the team event barren hunting ground for the British (fourth place leaving them just out of the medals). For her part Linda Savage found the event an enormous strain, and even though the shooters did their best to adopt a fairly laid-back approach, the itinerary of one target approximately every hour and a quarter was bound to create problems. Linda described the scene when it came to each turn to shoot as being incredibly noisy, with none of the hush which tends to fall on English grounds while shooting is in progress; the knowledge that huge sums of money were being wagered on every shot did nothing to ease the situation and she described ZZ competition as the most intense pressure she has experienced in clay shooting thus far. In Paris the shoot-on-your-own ZZ format was even more fraught than usual, the long lonely walk to the shooting station in front of a huge excited audience being guaranteed to increase the pressure. If that long walk teaches anything at all it is about missing: 'You have to learn to take a miss with dignity as you walk back,' she says.

The format was ten targets per day, and by the end of the first day there were only three women left – two Britons and a Frenchwoman – the four-miss elimination rule having weeded out the opposition. For Linda the second day therefore held the guarantee of at least a bronze medal, although in her eyes that would have been akin to failure after coming so far. The Frenchwoman missed her first target out, and as this was her fourth miss it left Linda to do battle with Kerry Dineage for the title. The crucial moment came when Kerry hit her target but the centre fell out of bounds, which gave Linda the opportunity to use her advantage of shooting first to maximum effect. When it was all over she professes to feeling no immediate elation, rather a desperate tiredness and a feeling of compassion for the distraught young woman she had beaten. Once home the pressure found release in sleep. Normally a light sleeper, she spent twelve hours at a time in bed; this went on for a fortnight before the effect of the pressure created by winning spent itself. Practising every Thursday at the West Kent Shooting School, Linda finds that all other disciplines have a fairly mediocre taint after shooting ZZ. More recently she became the first woman to shoot a straight ten in France, in competition at Le Touquet. Her shooting talent combined with the ability to withstand high-pressure situations has led to an approach for her to train at Olympic Trap – another of the pressure disciplines. The future seems an exciting one for Britain's latest European Champion.

19 *The Role of the Sponsor*

As clay shooting continues to grow, with newcomers swelling the numbers at all types of shoots throughout the country, so the gap between the upper and lower classes – in terms of ability – seems to widen. As has been discussed in Chapter 6, those who shoot clays at the highest level perform under considerable mental stress. But financial considerations also create stress of a different kind. Quite simply, if the shooter wishes to reach the top and stay there he will need to shoot constantly and regularly. This means that he is going to get through a great deal of money, paying for competition entries and ammunition, to say nothing of travelling expenses. Unless the rewards for success match the effort and expense paid out then the whole exercise can quickly become a recipe for bankruptcy, only the very well-off being able to keep up the pace. This has led to the creation of increasingly fabulous prize pools, and although some see it as a stigma currently blighting the sport, with a select band of top shooters chasing the big prizes, it is merely a reflection of the conditions affecting all major sports.

Sponsorship is vitally important in every sport at the highest level, whether it is for Football League Champions or some relatively unknown clay shooter. The principle is broadly the same, for without a hefty input from outside, the spectacle will be greatly reduced and ultimately the sport itself must suffer. Whether the modern sportsman likes it or not, money is the key to success in almost every case; no football team can succeed on a consistent basis without the cash to buy and pay the best players, and no clay shooter can succeed without the wherewithal to practise regularly. Sponsorship is, of course, greatly sought after and difficult to acquire. No sponsor wants to be associated with a losing product, so the shooter invariably needs to achieve success first out of his own pocket. Once this has been attained there is every chance that a sponsor will come in to share the limelight and see their product advertised on a nationwide basis. It is simple economics, every sponsor wanting value for money.

Today all the major shoots have a degree of input from sponsors, with shotgun manufacturers and vehicle dealers to the fore. Perhaps the two best-known sponsorship packages have been made available

The 1990 British Skeet Champion, Jim Munday, happy enough with his Beretta sponsored prize

Above right: Another happy Browning Loyalty Prize winner

by the big names in shotgun shooting – Browning and Gunmark (the importers of Beretta). Both run Loyalty Prize schemes on an annual basis, available at specified shoots to winning competitors using their company's products. Beretta gave away twenty-three guns during 1989 with a total value of £24,000; Browning for their part offered up to seventy-six guns during 1990, worth £91,580, the success or otherwise of Browning users determining the actual extent of the prizes. Big-money prizes are available at all the major championship shoots. In many cases sponsorship takes a joint form, Gunmark and Saab combining on a regular basis; elsewhere Browning links up with other manufacturers such as Daihatsu, Subaru and Isuzu, while Ford also come in with car prizes. Others, too, can occasionally be persuaded to up the stakes; Jack Daniels, Omega and a host of cartridge manufacturers such as Eley, Victory and RC all top up competitions.

Different manufacturers use a variety of sponsorship techniques. For example, Browning stay away from individual sponsorships, believing that their Loyalty Prize scheme is the best way of providing real incentive to Browning users on a nationwide basis rather than providing rich pickings for a handful of fortunate individuals. It follows that the man who makes the commitment to buy a Browning gun gives himself a continuing interest in staying with Browning by virtue of the substantial prizes on offer.

In order to get major benefit from their sponsorship packages, many of the larger companies now offer their own championships. Thus we see the Beretta World Sporting Championship, the Beretta Super Sporting Championship, the Club Beretta Championship, the

Browning DTL Championship, the Subaru DTL Championship, together with a host of others. Indeed, Browning sponsorship has influenced the format of the DTL championship weekends for both British and English Championships in recent times by providing an additional competition which has revitalised the events; in both cases the main event is followed by an additional hundred-bird championship on the following day – a popular and effective method of providing maximum benefit for the shooter in a neat format. In some cases the pot hunter will attempt to abuse the system by borrowing a gun in order to be eligible for a Loyalty Prize. This scarcely enters into the spirit of things, although such a shooter is less likely to make off with the spoils since by using a borrowed weapon he will in all probability shoot less well. On the other side of the coin, some shooters actually change permanently to a Beretta or Browning simply because of the fabulous prizes to be won, which far outstrip anything else on offer. The sponsors obviously feel that they get a good deal and the all-round effect is a positive one.

Sponsorship must have a high profile if it is to succeed

However, gun trade sponsorship is relatively poor compared with the sort of huge budgets which may be available from, say, a cigarette manufacturer, and without question the way forward is for shooters and shoot organisers to look outside the sport for extra sponsorship money. Where it succeeds this technique brings in additional cash while at the same time introducing shooting to non-shooters in a positive manner. Much good can come from the acquisition of sponsorship deals from outside the sport, and for the future we would all be well advised to cast the net a little wider than we do today.

20 The Future of Clay Shooting

In conclusion, it seems appropriate to consider some of the factors which must surely influence clay shooting during the 1990s and on into the twenty-first century. Will it prevail as a sport, and will it continue to blossom and flourish as it is doing at present? It is impossible to say, although there are certain factors which will undoubtedly affect the future of the sport. They include the public perception of shooting and shooters and how this may affect the right to own and use a shotgun; the environmental problem of lead pollution; the dearth of facilities due to planning constraints; and finally the constant spectre of noise pollution. It is a formidable list, but one which will not go away by our ignoring it.

PUBLIC PERCEPTION

The public perception of all shotgun shooting sports is of great importance. Unfortunately, the standing of the shotgun is not terribly high in the eyes of many members of the public, and this includes many 'nouveau' country dwellers as well as a great majority of town/city folk. Care for the environment is, of course, a noble cause; but far too many people don an environmentalist's mantle to camouflage blatant bias, and this can do much harm to the long-term aspirations of the shooting man. Public hysteria whipped up by an often ill-informed tabloid press has an enormous influence on the way administrations think and act. One of the most outstanding examples of the press influencing government was the change in the law which eventually saw the light of day in the Firearms (Amendment) Act, 1988. Many shooters felt that this Amendment was a direct result of public response to the horrific Hungerford massacre in which seventeen people, including the crazed gunman responsible for the outrage, lost their lives. Even though the murders were carried out with Part 1 Firearms, it was the ordinary shotgun owner who suffered the most from the measures brought into force following enactment.

As this incident proves, the whole future of shooting sports hangs perpetually in the balance, possibly subject to the whim of whatever maniac next happens to be abroad, and unquestionably dependent on public response. To those with a long history of shooting, the ownership and use of shotguns may seem to have changed only superficially. But in reality things are very different and for newcomers to the sport in particular there are significant hurdles to be scaled before any sport can be contemplated. In this the anti-shooting faction has won a substantial victory, one which was achieved with alarming ease and rapidity. Public response seldom takes account of logic, or even cold scientific fact, no matter how well presented, and here perhaps is the single largest potential influencing factor on how the sport will evolve over the next few decades.

LEAD SHOT

The use of lead in the environment, and the widespread acceptance of its undoubted polluting properties, is an issue which quite rightly is here to stay. At present it is lead in petrol that receives most public attention – if only because unleaded fuel is now a lot cheaper to buy – but the use of lead shot may also be seen as detrimental. Already the use of lead weights in coarse fishing has been banned; this has proved expensive but anglers have been able to adapt. There did seem to be an outstanding scientific case in support of such a ban, and few people argued in favour of polluting the nation's waterways and poisoning wildfowl. However, the same sort of scientific evidence against lead shot in shotgun cartridges does not exist, although from a general environmental standpoint few would be in favour of using lead if a viable alternative were to become available.

Despite their apparent similarity, lead shot for fishing and lead shot for shooting are a million miles apart. Of course, lead shot can pollute land under certain circumstances (although to what degree and with what longevity research does not as yet make clear), and none of us can favour that; but a balance needs to be struck, intensity of usage and long-term effects on land being important considerations. On the muddy foreshore of an estuary, lead shot will soon settle beyond the reach of any feeding birds, and is unlikely to disperse and enter the food chain through the mud itself; on firmer land the same may not apply, the area of fall of shot at major clay-shooting grounds being likely to receive tons of lead shot over a prolonged period. Can lead enter the food chain via this route, especially where land is grazed over by stock or where crops are grown? Ready answers are not yet available, though given time they doubtless will be. The poser is whether or not pressure groups will wait that long before hysteria begins to set in.

Steel shot is
possibly on the
way

Ballistics and effective killing power are obvious prime considerations for the shotgunner. At some point non-toxic materials are sure to become available, though only time will tell whether they will be an acceptable alternative to lead. The BASC leads the country in research in this area. At this stage steel seems unacceptable on the grounds of performance, and tungsten on the grounds of cost; but finding a solution should not prove beyond the wit of the cartridge manufacturers who stand to lose so much if the environmentalists beat them to the punch.

Quite how a change-over will affect clay shooting is impossible to say, but it is probably fair to assume that there is going to be an element of increased cost which will be passed on to the consumer, while there may also be a noticeable shortfall in terms of cartridge performance when compared with today's high-performance loads. Already the shooting authorities have made a contribution to a better environment by reducing competition loads to one ounce, and so long as the powers that be retain an open mind perhaps shooters will not be too badly served in the future.

PLANNING CONSENTS AND ENVIRONMENTAL HEALTH

One of the biggest bones of contention among both shooters and those on the periphery of the shooting scene is the scarcity of satisfactory

facilities. On the whole, the facilities in terms of layouts are adequate because the regulating bodies, usually the CPSA, dictate that layouts should be of a certain standard. Such facilities are widespread throughout the country and are of a largely uniform standard so that in this respect the shooter is well served. It is in the field of back-up facilities that the problem lies, many grounds still offering the bare minimum in terms of toilets and catering. Often it is money that is the problem, although just as frequently the issue is a far deeper one, unsympathetic local authorities being loath to provide the necessary consents. By and large local authorities nationwide seem to be less than helpful to the owners of shooting grounds; as clay shooting is one of the biggest up-and-coming leisure pursuits in the country this stance is somewhat surprising and difficult to explain. In all probability by making such a comment I run the risk of incurring the wrath of some pro-shooting council or other which has bent over backwards to assist shooters in its area. However, in terms of assistance to a boom sport, on average local authorities do seem inclined to turn a convenient deaf ear – at best – while pouring money into every other form of recreation imaginable.

Even where consents under the Town and Country Planning Acts are obtained, there will often be various conditions relating to usage, some of which quickly make many a new project uneconomic. Increasingly clay-shooting grounds are being run on a business footing, and any significant capital outlay needs to be justified before it

Shooting facilities may be first class, but often other facilities lag behind

169

can be seriously contemplated. Few would deny that better facilities in an area are a boon, yet the difficulties inherent in obtaining workable planning consents suggest that the official view is very different. The Town and Country Planning General Development Order 1977 (GDO) allows land to be used for unapproved activities for up to twenty-eight days in each year before a planning application becomes necessary, and it is a sad indictment of the system that the great majority of shooting grounds choose to operate within this GDO rather than run the risk of applying for planning consents which may open the door to restrictions. In 1989 the reduction in the number of days allowed under the GDO from twenty-eight to fourteen created an enormous furore in the shooting world, not least because it was done 'through the back door'. Fortunately the decision was reversed due to fierce pressure from shooters, and this counts as one of the most important victories for the shooting lobby in recent years. Had no reversal been achieved there can be little doubt that the effect on the sport would have been catastrophic: much shooting opportunity would have been lost with the number of available days slashed in half; many shooting grounds would have become uneconomic, while many more would have curtailed capital expenditure. Many shooters saw this as a further anti-shooting plot, coming so soon after the repressive legislation of the Firearms (Amendment) Act – and who can honestly say that such a view is totally wrong?

Even where planning consents are obtained by the applicant shooting ground, other factors may arise. Once again unsympathetic local authorities are held to blame by many shooters, with noise pollution being the stumbling block. Irrespective of planning consents, the Control of Pollution Act 1974 allows the Environmental Health Officer to apply enormous pressure to shooting grounds against whom there have been complaints. This really does call into question the efficacy of local authorities which first allow planning consents that permit and indeed encourage shooting-ground owners to invest heavily in their site, only for the Environmental Health Officer subsequently to come along and demand restrictions that make such investments uneconomic – even in extreme cases to close a site altogether. No amount of planning consents can override the Control of Pollution Act, and if we are honest none of us would wish to see it any other way. However, what are desperately needed are more sensible and workable ground rules to protect not only the local populace but also the shooters. Shooters also have rights, and among these is surely the right to have facilities suitable for pursuing their sport within reasonably comfortable striking distance of major centres of population. Unfortunately clay shooting is a noisy pastime, although whether it is excessively or offensively noisy is another matter. Quite clearly there need to be better parameters than the sensibilities of a small clique of local inhabitants, who may well be biased against shooting in the first place; as things stand complaints from even a single individual can bring down the full weight of the Environmental Health Officer against the supposed offenders even where the legitimacy of the complaint has yet to be established.

The CPSA has worked hard to produce an acceptable Code of Practice which will govern the amount of permissible noise that may be emitted by shooting grounds; this Code is presently the subject of consultation with the Department of the Environment, and its eventual adoption should do much to see a more even-handed approach to this undoubted problem. Some people may hold the view that council officers are too quick to jump, and would best serve the *whole* community by careful research and reasoned argument in advance of wielding the big stick. Unfortunately some shooting-ground owners have ruffled feathers and generally behaved in the sort of boorish manner which inevitably gets shooting a bad name; increasingly the rest of us have to pick up the tab for such behaviour, and this makes the fight ahead all the harder.

PROSPECTS

Despite such difficulties, the prospects in the years ahead are good so long as the sport can come to terms with the problems besetting it. The average clay shooter knows little of the 'heavy' issues, mentioned above, which are confronting the sport. This is as it should be, for after all the name of the game is enjoyment. Money *can* be made available for this growth sport: the Sports Council and local authorities can be persuaded to come up with fairly substantial amounts if approached in the proper manner. The preceding chapter illustrates the sort of commitment being made by the gun trade, and other commercial interests are also increasingly keen to see an input into the sport provided they can see a worthwhile return. Such a return may be deemed worthwhile only if the image of the sport is ultra-clean, the ultimate evolution perhaps being towards fewer but larger and better grounds. The face of clay shooting is constantly changing, and shooters would do well to consider the reasons for such changes as they occur. As with everything else, the future of the sport rests firmly in the hands of its administrators and participants, and so long as we respond positively to the changing political and economic climate then there need be no fears. Good shooting!

Glossary

averages average scores recorded for classification purposes.

barrel shotgun barrel.

bore inside measurement of the barrel.

choke constriction at end of barrels.

classification the alloted class in which each shooter will be placed according to his average attained during the previous period.

clay clay pigeon.

clays (birds) only non-competition entry.

English Skeet domestic version of Skeet.

English Sporting Sporting under English CPSA rules.

FITASC Sporting Sporting under FITASC rules.

gauge inside measurement of the barrel.

Gun the shooter.

gun weapon used.

High gun overall winner.

ISU Skeet international version of Skeet.

layout any clay pigeon set-up.

magazine the chamber for holding extra cartridges in a single-barrel gun.

muzzle barrel end.

pump gun gun with a repeating action operated by hand in pumping the forend.

recoil the rearward force imparted by a fired shotgun.

Registered competition run under the auspices/rules of the CPSA, with the scores being recorded for classification purposes.

safety catch device for preventing the gun from firing.

semi-auto gun with a repeating action operated by the built-in system within the gun.

Shot the shooter.

shot cartridge contents.

Skeet two different crossing targets on a fixed layout.

Sporting any permutation of differing targets.

stand firing position.

station firing position.

Trap all 'going away' disciplines (DTL, ABT and Trench).

trap clay pigeon launcher.

5-trap 5-trap Universal Trench.

15-trap 15-trap Olympic Trench (or Trap).

Bibliography

An Introduction to Clay Shooting by John Upton and Philip Fletcher (Argus Books, 1987)
Clay Pigeon Marksmanship by Percy Stanbury and Gordon Carlisle (Stanley Paul, 3rd edition 1974)
Clay Shooting by Peter Croft (Ward Lock, 1990)
Clay Target Shooting by Paul Bentley (A. & C. Black, 1987)
Sporting Clays by A.J. Smith (Argus Books, 1989)

Magazines

Clay Shooting (bi-monthly)
Pull! (monthly)
Shooting Magazine (monthly)
Shooting Times & Country Magazine (weekly)
Sporting Gun (monthly)

Index